JN102714

# ◆◆◆ 本書の構成と特色 ◆◆◆

本書は第一学習社発行の英文法準教科書『**Zoom English Grammar 23 Lessons THIRD EDITION**』に準拠したドリル形式のワークブックです。テキスト本体の練習問題を補充するとともに，テキストの基本的な文法事項が着実に定着するように編集しています。

## 【特色】

◆ドリル形式で同じパターンの問題を繰り返し練習できるようにしました。

◆基本的な文法事項が確実に身につくように，基礎的な問題を中心に構成しました。

◆テキスト本体の例文をそのまま使った問題には「★」印をつけ，重要な例文の理解に役立てるようにしました。

◆学習事項の要点がつかめるよう，また，練習のヒントにもなるよう，各問題に「ポイント」を設けました。

◆各問の指示文の末尾に，テキスト本体の項目との対応関係を「A」「B」などと示して，効果的に学習が進められるようにしました。

◆各レッスンの最後には，テキスト本体の各項目を横断した「総合」問題を設けました。

# ─── CONTENTS ───

# 動詞の変化ドリル

**1** 次の動詞に3人称・単数・現在の-s，-esをつけなさい。

① keep _____　② begin _____

③ drive _____　④ get _____

⑤ need _____　⑥ watch _____

⑦ finish _____　⑧ go _____

⑨ miss _____　⑩ fly _____

⑪ play _____　⑫ try _____

**ポイント**

ふつうの場合：-s
-s, -x, -sh, -chで
終わる語：-es
子音字＋y：yをiに
変えて-es
母音字＋y：-s

**2** 次の動詞を過去形にしなさい。

① look _____　② learn _____

③ hope _____　④ live _____

⑤ use _____　⑥ believe _____

⑦ enjoy _____　⑧ try _____

⑨ study _____　⑩ play _____

⑪ want _____　⑫ need _____

⑬ stop _____　⑭ plan _____

**ポイント**

ふつうの場合：-ed
-eで終わる語：-d
子音字＋y：yをiに
変えて-ed
母音字＋y：-ed
アクセントのある
1母音字＋1子音
字：子音字を重ねて
-ed

**3** 次の動詞を過去形にしなさい。

① speak _____　② have _____

③ tell _____　④ make _____

⑤ know _____　⑥ buy _____

⑦ give _____　⑧ find _____

⑨ understand _____　⑩ do _____

⑪ eat _____　⑫ get _____

**ポイント**

不規則な変化をする
動詞には大事なもの
が多いので，1つ1
つしっかり覚えてお
こう。

**4** 次の動詞を～ing形にしなさい。

① catch _____　② say _____

③ hear _____　④ think _____

⑤ become _____　⑥ ride _____

⑦ lose _____　⑧ die _____

⑨ lie _____　⑩ begin _____

⑪ forget _____　⑫ run _____

**ポイント**

ふつうの場合：-ing
子音字＋e：eを消
して-ing
-ieで終わる語：ie
をyに変えて-ing
アクセントのある
1母音字＋1子音
字：子音字を重ねて
-ing

# 比較変化ドリル

## 1 次の形容詞・副詞の比較級，最上級を書きなさい。

| | 比較級 | 最上級 |
|---|---|---|
| ① old | _____ | _____ |
| ② fast | _____ | _____ |
| ③ tall | _____ | _____ |
| ④ strong | _____ | _____ |
| ⑤ clean | _____ | _____ |
| ⑥ wide | _____ | _____ |
| ⑦ nice | _____ | _____ |
| ⑧ happy | _____ | _____ |
| ⑨ busy | _____ | _____ |
| ⑩ heavy | _____ | _____ |
| ⑪ hot | _____ | _____ |

> **ポイント**
> ふつうの場合：-er, -est
> -e で終わる語：e を消して-er, -est
> 子音字＋y：y を i に変えて-er, -est
> １母音字＋１子音字：子音字を重ねて-er, -est

## 2 次の形容詞・副詞の比較級，最上級を書きなさい。

| | 比較級 | 最上級 |
|---|---|---|
| ① important | _____ | _____ |
| ② famous | _____ | _____ |
| ③ useful | _____ | _____ |
| ④ exciting | _____ | _____ |
| ⑤ popular | _____ | _____ |
| ⑥ beautiful | _____ | _____ |
| ⑦ expensive | _____ | _____ |
| ⑧ interesting | _____ | _____ |
| ⑨ dangerous | _____ | _____ |
| ⑩ slowly | _____ | _____ |

> **ポイント**
> ２音節語の大部分と３音節以上の語：more-, most-
> -ly で終わる副詞：more-, most-

## 3 次の形容詞・副詞の比較級，最上級を書きなさい。

| | 比較級 | 最上級 |
|---|---|---|
| ① good | _____ | _____ |
| ② bad | _____ | _____ |
| ③ many | _____ | _____ |
| ④ ill | _____ | _____ |

> **ポイント**
> 不規則な変化をする形容詞・副詞は，１つ１つしっかり覚えておこう。

**1** 例にならい，次の文の後ろに（　）内の語句を加えて，過去を表す文にしなさい。　**A**

（例）It is very warm.　(yesterday)

　　→ It was very warm yesterday.

① We are late for school.　(this morning)

---

② His sister is very busy.　(at that time)

---

③ I am tired.　(last night)

---

④ He is very hungry.　(then)

---

⑤ My children are interested in the game.　(last year)

---

⑥ Tom is very angry at me.　(then)

---

| ポイント | | |
| --- | --- | --- |
| **be-動詞の過去形** | | |
| 現在 | | 過去 |
| am | → | was |
| is | → | was |
| are | → | were |

**2** 例にならい，日本文を参考に，次の文を否定文にしなさい。　**A**

（例）This is my bike.

　　→ This (isn't) my bike.　（これは私の自転車ではありません。）

① My uncle was a doctor.

　My uncle (　　　　　　) a doctor.

　（私のおじは医者ではありませんでした。）

② I am from Canada.

　I'm (　　　　　　) from Canada.

　（私はカナダ出身ではありません。）

★③ They are my classmates.

　They (　　　　　　) my classmates.

　（彼らは私のクラスメートではありません。）

④ These books were very interesting.

　These books (　　　　　　) very interesting.

　（これらの本はあまりおもしろくありませんでした。）

⑤ Japan is a very big country.

　Japan (　　　　　　) a very big country.

　（日本はあまり大きい国ではありません。）

| ポイント | | |
| --- | --- | --- |
| **be-動詞の否定形** | | |
| I am [I'm] | | |
| | → | I'm not |
| is | → | isn't |
| are | → | aren't |
| was | → | wasn't |
| were | → | weren't |

**3** 例にならい，（　　）内の語を主語にして文を書きかえなさい。　　B

ポイント
「3人称・単数・現在」は動詞に -s, -es をつける。

(例)　I wash my hair every morning.　(she)

　　　→ She washes her hair every morning.

① I keep my CDs in a box.　(he)

　_____ his CDs in a box.

② Jim and Ken have a lot of books.　(Jim)

　_____ a lot of books.

③ The boys finish their homework before dinner.　(the boy)

　_____ his homework before dinner.

④ Kenji and Yuka fly to New York every summer.　(Yuka)

　_____ to New York every summer.


**4** 例にならい，次の文に（　　）内の語句を加えて，過去形の文にしなさい。　　B

ポイント
一般動詞の過去形
-ed, -d をつけるものと，不規則な変化をするものがある。

(例)　I study Chinese with Keiko.　(last night)

　　　→ I studied Chinese with Keiko last night.

① Bill lives in Kyoto.　(seven years ago)

　------------------------------------------------

② My aunt arrives at the airport.　(twenty minutes ago)

　------------------------------------------------

③ It rains a lot in summer.　(in 2002)

　------------------------------------------------

④ A stranger speaks to me in English at the corner of a street.

　　　　　　　　　　　　　　　　　　　(yesterday)

　------------------------------------------------

⑤ We leave home at eight.　(this morning)

　------------------------------------------------


**5** 例にならい，次の文を否定文にしなさい。　　B

ポイント
一般動詞の文の否定文
現在：
don't [doesn't] ＋動詞の原形
過去：
didn't＋動詞の原形

(例)　You like English.

　　　→ You (don't) (like) English.

① John needs this key.

　John (　　　　　) (　　　　　　) this key.

② They went to Canada.

　They (　　　　　) (　　　　　　) to Canada.

③ Those girls play the piano.

　Those girls (　　　　　) (　　　　　　) the piano.

④ Mr. Kato spoke loudly.

　Mr. Kato (　　　　　) (　　　　　　) loudly.

**6** 例にならい，次の文を疑問文にしなさい。また，疑問文への答えも書きなさい。 **C**

(例)　You are an exchange student.

　　→ (Are) (you) an exchange student? —— Yes, (I) (am).

　　You play basketball every day.

　　→ (Do) you (play) basketball every day? —— Yes, (I) (do).

**ポイント**

**be-動詞の文の疑問文**
主語　＋be-動詞.

Be-動詞＋主語 ...?

**一般動詞の文の疑問文**
現在：
Do [Does]＋主語
　＋動詞の原形 ...?
過去：
Did＋主語＋動詞
　の原形 ...?

① This is Tom's notebook.

　(　　　　　) (　　　　　　　　) Tom's notebook?

　—— No, (　　　　　　) (　　　　　　　).

② That book was interesting.

　(　　　　　) (　　　　　) (　　　　　　　) interesting?

　—— Yes, (　　　　　　) (　　　　　　).

③ The girls were absent from school.

　(　　　　　) (　　　　　) (　　　　　　) absent from school?

　—— No, (　　　　　　) (　　　　　　).

④ She likes you.

　(　　　　　) she (　　　　　) you?

　—— Yes, (　　　　　　) (　　　　　　).

⑤ That cat runs very fast.

　(　　　　　) that cat (　　　　　) very fast?

　—— No, (　　　　　　) (　　　　　　).

★⑥ You like our school.

　(　　　　　) you (　　　　　) our school?

　—— Yes, (　　　　　　) (　　　　　　).

⑦ Mika and Yoko went shopping last weekend.

　(　　　　　) Mika　and　Yoko (　　　　　　) shopping　last

　weekend?

　—— No, (　　　　　　) (　　　　　　).

**総合** 日本文の意味に合うように，(　　　)内の語句を並べかえて，文を完成させなさい。

① この前の日曜日はとても天気がよかった。

(was / the weather / very nice) last Sunday.

------

② ユミコは昨夜，台所で皿洗いをしました。

(Yumiko / the dishes / washed / in the kitchen) last night.

------

③ あなたのお父さんは英語を話しますか。

(speak / your father / English / does)?

------

**5**

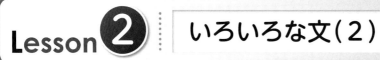
**1** 日本文を参考に，空所に適語を補いなさい。 **A**

① (　　　　　　　) did he buy the desk?

（彼はいつその机を買ったのですか。）

② (　　　　　　　) does it mean? （それはどういう意味ですか。）

③ (　　　　　　　) is that tall man? （あの背の高い男性はだれですか。）

④ (　　　　　　　) did you ask him such a question?

（あなたはなぜそんな質問を彼にしたのですか。）

★⑤ (　　　　　　　) is your favorite subject?

（好きな科目は何ですか。）

⑥ (　　　　　) (　　　　　) (　　　　　) does the boat

carry?

（そのボートは何台の車を運びますか。）

⑦ (　　　　　　　) ate my chocolate?

（だれが私のチョコレートを食べたのですか。）

> **ポイント**
>
> who（だれ）/ what（何）/ which（どちら，どれ）/ when（いつ）/ where（どこ）/ why（なぜ）/ how（どのようにして）/ how many（どのくらい…か）

**2** 日本文を参考に，空所に適語を補いなさい。 **B**

① Mary is your friend, (　　　　　) (　　　　　)?

（メアリーはあなたの友だちですよね。）

―― Yes, she (　　　　　). （はい，そうです。）

② Tom isn't your classmate, (　　　　　) (　　　　　)?

（トムはあなたのクラスメートではないよね。）

―― No, he (　　　　　). （はい，違います。）

③ Your grandmother was a good cook, (　　　　　) (　　　　　)?

（あなたのおばあさんは料理が上手だったよね。）

―― Yes, (　　　　　) (　　　　　). （はい，そうでした。）

④ You like soccer, (　　　　　) (　　　　　)?

（あなたはサッカーが好きですよね。）

―― Yes, (　　　　　) (　　　　　). （はい，好きです。）

⑤ Tom and Ken don't get up early, (　　　　　) (　　　　　)?

（トムとケンは早起きではありませんよね。）

―― Yes, (　　　　　) (　　　　　). （いいえ，早起きです。）

⑥ The man doesn't look busy, (　　　　　) (　　　　　)?

（その人は忙しそうには見えませんね。）

―― (　　　　　), (　　　　　) (　　　　　). （はい，見えません。）

> **ポイント**
>
> **付加疑問文**
> 「…ですよね」
> 　肯定文, 否定形＋主語？
> 「…ではありませんよね」
> 　否定文, 肯定形＋主語？

**3** 例にならい，命令文を作りなさい。 **C**

(例) You don't study hard. → Study hard.
      You use my pen. → Don't use my pen.

① You're not kind to old people.

----

② You watch TV too much.

----

③ You don't get up early.

----

④ You are noisy here.

----

⑤ You come home late.

----

⑥ You don't finish your work in time.

----

⑦ You don't go to the dentist.

----

**4** 日本文を参考に，空所に How か What を入れて感嘆文を完成させなさい。 **C**

① (　　　　　　) beautiful that picture is!
(あの絵はなんてきれいなのだろう。)

★② (　　　　　　) beautiful her voice is!
(彼女の声はなんてきれいなのでしょう。)

③ (　　　　　　) delicious coffee this is!
(これはなんておいしいコーヒーなのだろう。)

④ (　　　　　　) well she plays the guitar!
(彼女はなんて上手にギターを弾くのでしょう。)

⑤ (　　　　　　) a good guitarist she is!
(彼女はなんて上手にギターを弾くのでしょう。)

⑥ (　　　　　　) wonderful our world is!
(私たちの世界はなんてすばらしいのでしょう。)

⑦ (　　　　　　) fast cars those are!
(あれらはなんて速い車なのでしょう。)

**総合** 空所に適語を補って，対話文を完成させなさい。

① *A:* He doesn't like pizza, does he?　*B:* No, (　　　　　) (　　　　　　).

② *A:* (　　　　　) do you like, summer or winter?　*B:* I like summer.

③ *A:* (　　　　　) are you crying?　*B:* Because I lost my wallet.

# Lesson ③ 文の型（1）

●参考書 p.51-55
●文法書 p.10-11

**1** 例にならい，次の文の主語に＿＿を，述語動詞に～～を引きなさい。 **A**

（例） Our school starts at eight forty every day.

① Children in the world play with dolls.

② The beautiful lady came here with Peter.

③ Every morning, my brother walks to his office.

④ The earth moves around the sun.

⑤ That new shop at the corner opens at nine.

⑥ The old man died the day before yesterday.

⑦ These flowers grow quickly.

★⑧ Many people in our town work in the factory.

⑨ Last summer, the famous singer stayed at this hotel.

⑩ The plane arrived at the airport half an hour ago.

> **ポイント**
> まず述語動詞が何であるかに注目する。動詞を見つけたら，それより前にある名詞を見つける。

**2** 例にならい，日本文を参考に，[　]内から適切な動詞を選んで補いなさい。 **B**

（例） This orange (tastes) sweet. （このオレンジは甘い。）
[feels / smells / tastes / sounds]

① Leaves (　　　　　　) red and yellow in fall.
（秋には木の葉は紅葉します。） [become / turn / grow / come]

② He (　　　　　　) silent during the meeting.
（彼は会議の間黙っていた。） [grew / kept / seemed / sounded]

★③ I sometimes (　　　　　　) very hungry in the morning.
（私はときどき午前中にとてもおなかがすきます。）
[grow / turn / make / get]

④ She (　　　　　　) very busy. （彼女はとても忙しそうに見えた。）
[saw / looked / made / became]

⑤ Her story didn't (　　　　　　) true then.
（彼女の話はそのとき本当のようには聞こえなかった。）
[hear / listen / think / sound]

⑥ This rose (　　　　　　) so sweet.
（このバラはとても甘い香りがする。）
[feels / smells / tastes / sounds]

⑦ Your father (　　　　　　) very young.
（あなたのお父さんはとても若く見えます。）
[looks / becomes / gets / comes]

> **ポイント**
> 「**S＋V＋C**」の文型に使われる主な動詞
> appear, look, seem ;
> keep, stay, remain ;
> become, get, grow, turn ;
> feel, smell, taste, sound

**3** 日本文の意味に合うように，（　　）内の語句を並べかえて，文を完成させなさい。　C

ポイント
S+V+O
「SはOをVする」
動詞の後に目的語が
くる。

★① 私たちは月曜日から土曜日までサッカーをします。

(play / soccer / we) from Monday to Saturday.

② ジェーンは札幌でたくさんの写真を撮った。

(a lot of pictures / Jane / took) in Sapporo.

③ 私たちは昨日の午後，駅でその先生に会った。

(we / the teacher / met) at the station yesterday afternoon.

④ 私はそのパーティーで楽しい時を過ごした。

(a good time / had / I) at the party.

⑤ トムと私はときどきこの部屋でピアノを弾きます。

(Tom and I / the piano / sometimes play) in this room.

⑥ あなたはどこでその時計を買ったのですか。

Where (buy / the watch / did / you)?

**4** 下線部の語句が目的語か補語かを答えなさい。　B C

① It was cold yesterday.　（　　　　　　）
② The man smelled this apple.　（　　　　　　）
③ This apple smells sweet.　（　　　　　　）
④ She got the Nobel prize.　（　　　　　　）
⑤ I played the violin with him in this room.　（　　　　　　）
⑥ Why do you need a car?　（　　　　　　）
⑦ Their son became an actor.　（　　　　　　）

ポイント
S+V+O
S≠Oの関係
（OはVの動作の対
象）
S+V+C
S＝Cの関係

**総合** 日本文の意味に合うように，（　　）内の語句を並べかえて，文を完成させなさい。

① 私たちの前の車が突然止まった。　(in front of us / the car / stopped) suddenly.

② このミルクはあまりいい味がしない。　(this milk / very good / doesn't taste).

③ 私たちはこの町の人をたくさんは知りません。

(we / in this town / many people / don't know).

# Lesson 4 文の型（2）

参考書 p.56-61
文法書 p.12-13

**1** 例にならい，日本文を参考に，[　]内の語を適切な場所に入れて，全文を書きなさい。　**A**

（例）　Tom gave some flowers.　[his mother]

（トムは母親に花をあげた。）

→ Tom gave his mother some flowers.

> **ポイント**
>
> **S＋V＋O₁（間接目的語）＋O₂（直接目的語）**
> 「SはO₁にO₂をVする」
> Vの後に2つの目的語がくる。

① My aunt sent a Christmas card.　[me]

（私のおばはクリスマスカードを私に送ってくれた。）

② Please show your notebook.　[us]

（私たちにあなたのノートを見せてください。）

③ Jim found a nice seat.　[Mary]

（ジムはメアリーにいい席を見つけてあげた。）

④ Does your sister cook breakfast?　[you]

（あなたのお姉さんはあなたに朝食を作ってくれますか。）

⑤ Our teacher sometimes tells interesting stories.　[us]

（私たちの先生はときどきおもしろい話を私たちにしてくれる。）

**2** 例にならい，次の文の動詞に注意して第3文型（S＋V＋O）の文に書きかえなさい。　**A**

（例）　Please pass me the salt. → Please pass the salt to me.

My father bought me a computer.

→ My father bought a computer for me.

> **ポイント**
>
> O₁とO₂の順序を逆にしたときに，to＋O₁となる動詞と，for＋O₁となる動詞がある。
> **to ...**：give, hand, lend, pass, pay, sell, send, show, teach, tell
> **for ...**：buy, build, choose, cook, find, get, make

① He made her some sandwiches.

★② Our coach gives us good advice.

③ Father taught us mathematics.

④ Meg doesn't tell her mother the truth.

⑤ Let's find your daughter a nice present.

**3** 例にならい，S＋V＋O＋Cの文を作りなさい。　**B**

(例)　I call _____.　(Rose / my dog)

　　→ I call <u>my dog Rose</u>.

① Jack painted _____.　(his house / white)

--------------------------------------------------

★② Music makes _____.　(happy / me)

--------------------------------------------------

③ Leave _____.　(open / the window)

--------------------------------------------------

④ I can't get _____.　(warm / my hands)

--------------------------------------------------

⑤ May I call _____?　(Jenny / you)

--------------------------------------------------

> **ポイント**
> **S＋V＋O＋C**
> 「SはOをCに[であると]Vする」
> O＝Cの関係が成り立つ。

**4**　下線部の語句が目的語か補語かを答えなさい。　**A** **B**

① She found the book <u>easy</u>.　(　　　　　)
② She found him <u>the book</u>.　(　　　　　)
③ My friends call me <u>Ken</u>.　(　　　　　)
④ He made his sons <u>new desks</u>.　(　　　　　)
⑤ Tom always keeps his room <u>clean</u>.　(　　　　　)

> **ポイント**
> **S＋V＋O₁＋O₂**
> O₁≠O₂の関係
> **S＋V＋O＋C**
> O＝Cの関係

**5**　日本文の意味に合うように，(　　)内の語句を並べかえて，文を完成させなさい。　**C**

① かごには5羽の鳥がいます。　There (are / in the cage / five birds).
　There _____.
② テーブルの下にかぎがあります。　There (is / under the table / a key).
　There _____.
③ 公園には何匹か犬がいました。　There (some dogs / were / in the park).
　There _____.
④ ドアのところに猫がいます。　There (at the door / is / a cat).
　There _____.

> **ポイント**
> **There＋be-動詞＋**
> **S ...**
> 「…にSがいる[ある]」
> be-動詞の後にくる主語に合わせて動詞の形を変化させる。

**総合**　日本文の意味に合うように，空所に適語を補いなさい。

① 彼女は息子にスケートボードを買ってあげた。
　She (　　　　　　　) a skateboard (　　　　　　　) her son.
② 両親は赤ちゃんをダニエルと名づけた。
　The parents (　　　　　　　) their baby Daniel.
③ 私の家の近くに新しい店があります。
　(　　　　　　　) (　　　　　　　) a new shop near my house.

**1** 例にならい，（　　）内の動詞を現在時制か現在進行形にして，全文を書きなさい。また，日本語に訳しなさい。　A

（例）　She (like) Japanese pop music.

　　➔ She likes Japanese pop music.

　　（彼女は日本のポピュラー音楽が好きです。）

★① They (jog) in the park every morning.

訳：

② The moon (rise) in the east.

訳：

③ Where is Naomi? ── She (study) in her room.

訳：

④ The baby (cry) because it is hungry now.

訳：

> **ポイント**
> **現在時制**
> 現在を中心として，過去から未来にわたることがらを表す。
> **現在進行形**
> 今だけの進行中の動作を表す。

**2** 例にならい，now を後ろにつけて，現在進行形の文にしなさい。　A

（例）　I play tennis. ➔ I am playing tennis now.

① My dogs run in the garden.

★② I swim at a beach in Okinawa.

③ John takes a walk in the park.

④ Jim does his homework.

⑤ They don't listen to the radio.

⑥ Mr. Brown doesn't watch television.

⑦ Does Hideki play a video game?

> **ポイント**
> **現在進行形**
> 「～している」
> am [are, is] ＋～ing
> 否定文は am not
> [aren't, isn't] ＋～ing

**3** 例にならい，（　）内の動詞を過去時制か過去進行形にして，全文を書きなさい。　B

（例）　Tom (listen) to music when I (visit) him.

　　→ Tom was listening to music when I visited him.

① When Tom (arrive), we (have) dinner.

------------------------------------------------

★② Steve (read) a book when the phone (ring).

------------------------------------------------

③ It (not rain) when she (go) out.

------------------------------------------------

④ When I (enter) the room, he (talk) on the telephone.

------------------------------------------------

ポイント

過去時制
過去のある期間にわたる状態・習慣的な動作や，完結した動作を表す。

過去進行形
過去のある時点で進行していた動作を表す。

**4** 例にならい，次の文の後ろに（　）内の語句を加えて，過去進行形の文にしなさい。　B

（例）　It rained heavily.　(at that time)

　　→ It was raining heavily at that time.

① My husband wrote to our daughter.　(then)

------------------------------------------------

② Mary and Ichiro studied math.　(at that time)

------------------------------------------------

③ They ate lunch in the restaurant.　(at one thirty yesterday)

------------------------------------------------

④ Did she look at the picture?　(at that time)

------------------------------------------------

⑤ Ms. Nakamura didn't cook.　(when he came)

------------------------------------------------

⑥ What did you do in the room?　(then)

------------------------------------------------

⑦ Did she dance with him?　(when you arrived at the party)

------------------------------------------------

ポイント

過去進行形
「〜していた」
was [were] ＋〜ing
否定文は wasn't [weren't] ＋〜ing

**総合** [　]内の動詞を適切な形にして空所に補い，対話文を完成させなさい。

① A: Excuse me, but you (　　　　　) (　　　　　) on my foot.　[stand]

　 B: Oh, I'm sorry.

② A: What (　　　　　) you (　　　　　) at nine last night?　[do]

　 B: I was watching a DVD.

③ A: Where are the children?

　 B: They (　　　　　) (　　　　　) in the garden.　[play]

**13**

# Lesson ⑥ 未来

参考書 p.78-80
文法書 p.18-19

**1** 例にならい，（　）内の語句を加えて，will を使った文にしなさい。　A

（例）　It is cloudy.　(tomorrow)

　　　→ It will be cloudy tomorrow.

① We know the result.　(tomorrow)

_____

② The baby sleeps well.　(soon)

_____

★③ I lend you my new CD.　(tomorrow)

_____

④ It snows around here.　(tomorrow evening)

_____

⑤ Jane doesn't enjoy our concert.　(tomorrow)

_____

⑥ How old is your brother?　(next year)

_____

> **ポイント**
> **will を使った未来の表現**
> 主語が何であっても「will ＋動詞の原形」の形は変わらない。
> 疑問文：
> 　Will ＋主語＋動詞の原形 ...?

**2** 例にならい，与えられた語句を用いて be going to を使った文を作りなさい。　B

（例）　I / buy a new car / next year

　　　→ I am going to buy a new car next year.

① it / rain / tomorrow

_____

② Ken / come here / next week

_____

③ I / buy some books / tomorrow

_____

④ I / take Alice to the museum / next month

_____

⑤ I / wear this dress to the party / this evening

_____

⑥ we / invite John to the party / next weekend

_____

⑦ I / play tennis with Jane / tomorrow

_____

> **ポイント**
> **be going to ～による未来の表現**
> be-動詞の形は主語に合わせて変わる。
> I am going to ～.
> He [She, It] is going to ～.
> You [We, They] are going to ～.

**3** 例にならい，次の文を疑問文にしなさい。また，疑問文への答えも書きなさい。　B

(例)　You are going to visit Hiroshima this summer.

→ <u>Are you going to visit</u> Hiroshima this summer?

―― Yes, I (am).

① They are going to join her birthday party.

_____ her birthday party?

―― Yes, they (　　　　　　).

② We are going to climb Mt. Fuji next week.

_____ Mt. Fuji next week?

―― Yes, we (　　　　　　).

③ Mr. Johnson is going to visit Chicago next month.

_____ Chicago next month?

―― No, he (　　　　　　).

④ Mike and Tom are going to play the guitar on the stage.

_____ the guitar on the stage?

―― No, they (　　　　　　).

**4** 日本文の意味に合うように，（　　）内の語句を並べかえて，文を完成させなさい。　C

① 文化祭は来週の金曜日に始まります。

(begins / next Friday / our school festival).

-----------------------------------------------

② この電車は何時に東京に着きますか。

What time (this train / Tokyo / does / get to)?

-----------------------------------------------

③ 私たちは来週の土曜日にパーティーを開くことになっています。

(we / are / a party / having) next Saturday.

-----------------------------------------------

**総合**　日本文の意味に合うように，空所に適語を補いなさい。

① 母親：この手紙はだれが出してくれるのかしら。　　息子：ぼくが出すよ。

*Mother:* Who (　　　　　　) post this letter for me?

*Son:* I (　　　　　　).

② *A:* あなたの自転車はパンクしています。　*B:* 知っています。明日修理するつもりです。

*A:* Your bike has a flat tire.

*B:* I know. I (　　　　　) (　　　　　) (　　　　　　) repair it tomorrow.

③ *A:* 玄関にだれかがいます。　*B:* 私が行ってドアを開けましょう。

*A:* There is somebody at the hall door.

*B:* I (　　　　　) go and open it.

# Lesson **7**  現在完了形

●参考書 p.81-84
○文法書 p.20-21

**1** 例にならい，[　　]内の語を使って現在完了形の文を作りなさい。また，その否定文と疑問文を作りなさい。　A

(例)　They (have) (taken) a bath. [take]
　　　否定文：They (haven't) (taken) a bath.
　　　疑問文：(Have) they (taken) a bath?

> **ポイント**
> **現在完了形**
> have [has] ＋過去分詞
> 否定文：
> 　haven't [hasn't] ＋
> 　過去分詞
> 疑問文：
> 　Have [Has] ＋主語
> 　＋過去分詞 ...?

① Your brother (　　　　　) (　　　　　　　) a new car. [buy]
　　否定文：Your brother (　　　　　) (　　　　　　) a new car.
　　疑問文：(　　　　　　) your brother (　　　　　) a new car?
② Robert (　　　　　) (　　　　　　) back home. [go]
　　否定文：Robert (　　　　　) (　　　　　) back home.
　　疑問文：(　　　　　) Robert (　　　　　) back home?
③ We (　　　　) (　　　　　) all the party food. [eat]
　　否定文：We (　　　　　) (　　　　　) all the party food.
　　疑問文：(　　　　　) you (　　　　　) all the party food?

**2** [　　]内の語を使って現在完了形の文を作り，対話文を完成させなさい。　A

① *A:* Yumi is charming, isn't she? I like her.
　　(ユミは魅力的だよね。ぼくは好きだよ。)
　*B:* You are too late. I (　　　　　) (　　　　　　) (　　　　　)
　　a date with her. [already / get]
　　(遅すぎるよ。ぼくはもう彼女とデートしたよ。)

> **ポイント**
> **完了・結果**
> 「～してしまった」
> just(ついさっき)，
> already(もう)，yet
> (疑問文で「もう」，
> 否定文で「まだ」)な
> どの語句を伴うこと
> が多い。

② *A:* Will you return the money?　(あのお金，返してくれないか。)
　*B:* What? I (　　　　　) (　　　　　　) (　　　　　　) it to
　　you. [already / return]　(何だって？　もう返したよ。)
③ *A:* I have to tell Tom to come here tomorrow.
　　(トムに明日ここへ来るよう伝えないと。)
　*B:* I (　　　　　) (　　　　　　) (　　　　　　) him about it.
　　[just / call]　(ついさっき電話したところだよ。)
④ *A:* Can I see your sister?　(きみのお姉さんと会えるかなあ。)
　*B:* She (　　　　　) (　　　　　　) (　　　　　　) out.
　　[just / go]　(さっき外出したところだ。)

**3** 例にならい，現在完了形の疑問文を作りなさい。また，その問いに対する答えを（　　　）内の日本語を参考にして完成させなさい。　**B**

（例）　How many times (have) (you) (visited) Kyoto? （2回）
　　　　── I have visited Kyoto (twice).

★① How many times (　　　　　) (　　　　　) (　　　　　)
　　a horse? （1回）── I have ridden a horse (　　　　　).

② How many times (　　　　　) (　　　　　) (　　　　　) to
　　Disneyland? （3回）── I have been there (　　　　　) times.

③ How many times (　　　　　) (　　　　　) (　　　　　)
　　that mountain? （1度もない）── I have (　　　　　) climbed it.

④ How many times (　　　　　) (　　　　　) (　　　　　)
　　to Jane? （しばしば）── I have (　　　　　) spoken to her.

**ポイント**

経験
「～したことがある」
ever（かつて），never
（一度も…ない），
before（以前に），
often（しばしば），
once（一度），twice
（二度），three times
（三度）などの語句を
伴うことが多い。

**4** 例にならい，（　　　）内に適語を補いなさい。〈　　　〉内の語は，適切なほうを選びなさい。　**C**

（例）　Do you know Bill?
　　　　── Yes, I (have) (known) him 〈for〉 a long time.

① Is Mary a teacher?
　　── Yes, she (　　　　　) (　　　　　) a teacher 〈since / for〉
　　two years.

② Are Mike and Beth in Japan?
　　── Yes, they (　　　　　) (　　　　　) there 〈since / for〉 1998.

③ Are you waiting for John?
　　── Yes, I (　　　　　) (　　　　　) waiting for him 〈since /
　　for〉 half an hour.

④ Is your mother working in the garden?
　　── Yes, she (　　　　　) (　　　　　) working in the garden
　　〈since / for〉 this morning.

**ポイント**

継続
「（今まで）ずっと…
だ」
since＋時の一点
for＋時の長さ

現在完了進行形
動作の継続（「ずっ
と～している」）は
have [has] been
～ingで表す。

**総合**　日本文の意味に合うように，空所に適語を補いなさい。

① A: 宿題はもう終えましたか。　　B: いいえ，まだです。
　　A: Have you (　　　　　) your homework (　　　　　)?
　　B: No, I haven't.

② A: 今までに北海道に行ったことはありますか。　　B: 一度行ったことがあります。
　　A: Have you ever (　　　　　) (　　　　　) Hokkaido?
　　B: Yes, I've been there (　　　　　).

③ A: とても暑いですね。　　B: ええ，1週間ずっと暑いです。
　　A: It's very hot, isn't it?
　　B: Yes, it (　　　　　) (　　　　　) very hot (　　　　　) a week.

**1** 例にならい，（　　）内に適語を補って過去完了形の文を作りなさい。　Ａ

（例）　The bus left.

→ The bus (had) (left) when I got to the bus stop.

① The baby fell asleep.

The baby (　　　　　) (　　　　　　　) asleep when her mother

got home.

② The concert started.

The concert (　　　　　　) (　　　　　　　) when I arrived.

③ She didn't read the newspaper.

She (　　　　　) (　　　　　　　) the newspaper yet when I saw

her yesterday morning.

④ The lesson began.

The lesson (　　　　　　) already (　　　　　　) when she

entered the classroom.

⑤ John had dinner.

John (　　　　　) (　　　　　　　) dinner when his parents got

home.

⑥ Mike learned Japanese.

Mike (　　　　　) (　　　　　　　) Japanese when he went to

live in Japan.

**2** 例にならい，過去完了進行形の文を作りなさい。　Ａ

（例）　Tom / work for the company / for ten years

→ Tom had been working for the company for ten years.

① Ken / work for a foreign bank / till 1999

② the patient / wait in the room / for an hour

③ Cathy / swim in the pool / since morning

④ the baby / cry loudly / before he fell asleep

⑤ Emi / study mathematics / for five hours

**3** 例にならい，日本文を参考に，（　　　）内の動詞の一方を過去形に，もう一方を過去完了形に直して全文を書きなさい。　B

(例)　We (eat) the cookie which she (make).
　　　(私たちは彼女が作ってくれていたクッキーを食べた。)
　　　→ We (ate) the cookie which she (had made).

① They (go) home after they (finish) their work.
　　(彼らは仕事を終えてから帰宅した。)

- - - - - - - - - - - - - - - - - - - - - - - - - - - - - - - - - - - - - - - - - -

★② He (give) her a pendant which he (buy) in Paris.
　　(彼は彼女に，パリで買ったペンダントをあげた。)

- - - - - - - - - - - - - - - - - - - - - - - - - - - - - - - - - - - - - - - - - -

③ I (be) happy to hear that my favorite team (win) the game.
　　(私はお気に入りのチームが試合に勝ったことを聞いてうれしかった。)

- - - - - - - - - - - - - - - - - - - - - - - - - - - - - - - - - - - - - - - - - -

④ Yesterday, I (find) the key you (are) looking for.
　　(昨日，私はあなたが探していたかぎを見つけました。)

- - - - - - - - - - - - - - - - - - - - - - - - - - - - - - - - - - - - - - - - - -

> **ポイント**
> **過去時制と過去完了形**
> 過去完了形は過去時制よりも前の「時」を表す。

**4** 例にならい，下線部の動詞を過去形にして全文を書きなさい。　B

(例)　Mr. Suzuki <u>thinks</u> that he is wrong.
　　　→ Mr. Suzuki thought that he was wrong.

① Ken <u>says</u> that he will run faster than Tom.

- - - - - - - - - - - - - - - - - - - - - - - - - - - - - - - - - - - - - - - - - -

② I <u>know</u> that his story wasn't true.

- - - - - - - - - - - - - - - - - - - - - - - - - - - - - - - - - - - - - - - - - -

③ Mary <u>tells</u> me that she has seen a tiger once.

- - - - - - - - - - - - - - - - - - - - - - - - - - - - - - - - - - - - - - - - - -

④ I <u>am</u> sure that she can do the work alone.

- - - - - - - - - - - - - - - - - - - - - - - - - - - - - - - - - - - - - - - - - -

> **ポイント**
> **時制の一致**
> 主節の動詞が過去になると従属節の動詞の時制も変化する。
>
> 現在時制→過去時制
> will → would
> can → could
>
> 現在進行形
> 　→ 過去進行形
>
> 過去時制
> 　→ 過去完了形
>
> 現在完了形
> 　→ 過去完了形

**総合**　日本文の意味に合うように，空所に適語を補いなさい。

① 私がホールに着いたときには，コンサートはもう始まっていた。
　　The concert (　　　　　　) (　　　　　　　) when I arrived at the hall.

② ジョンは日本に行ったことがないと言った。
　　John said that he (　　　　　　) never (　　　　　　) to Japan.

③ 家は静かだった。みんな寝てしまっていたのだ。
　　The house (　　　　　　) quiet.　Everybody (　　　　　　) (　　　　　　) to bed.

**1** 例にならい，次の文の下線部の動詞に can をつけて，全文を書きかえなさい。 **A**

（例） Cats see in the dark. → Cats can see in the dark.

① I speak Spanish well.

② The student runs one hundred meters in eleven seconds.

③ Linda dances the best of all the girls.

④ David answers such a difficult question.

⑤ She rides a horse.

⑥ May speaks five languages.

⑦ The little boy runs ten kilometers.

⑧ You see Mt. Fuji from this room.

> **ポイント**
> **助動詞**
> 「助動詞＋動詞の原形」で動詞にさまざまな意味をつけ加える。

**2** 例にならい，次の文を疑問文と否定文にしなさい。 **A**

（例） Bill can eat sushi. → 疑問文：Can Bill eat sushi?
　　　　　　　　　　　　　　 否定文：Bill can't eat sushi.

★① You can swim.

　疑問文：

　否定文：

② His wife can drive a car.

　疑問文：

　否定文：

③ Her sisters can ski well.

　疑問文：

　否定文：

④ His son can play chess.

　疑問文：

　否定文：

> **ポイント**
> **助動詞の文の疑問文**
> 助動詞＋主語＋動詞の原形 ...?
> **助動詞の文の否定文**
> 主語＋助動詞＋not 動詞の原形 ...

**3** 例にならい，次の文の下線部に Can I か Can you を補って，文を完成させなさい。　A

ポイント
**Can I ~?**
「～してもいいですか」と許可を求める。
**Can you ~?**
「～してくれませんか」と依頼する。

（例）　（訪問先でお手洗いを借りようとして）

<u>Can I</u> use the bathroom?

（荷物をたくさん持っている人がドアのそばに立っている人に向かって）

<u>Can you</u> open the door for me?

① （時間を知りたくて，時計を持っている人に対して）

＿＿＿＿＿＿＿＿＿＿ tell me the time, please?

② （レストランで店員が客に向かって）

＿＿＿＿＿＿＿＿＿＿ take your order?

③ （靴屋で客が店員に）

＿＿＿＿＿＿＿＿＿＿ try these shoes on?

④ （ラジオを消してほしいときに）

＿＿＿＿＿＿＿＿＿＿ turn off the radio?

⑤ （鉛筆を借りたいときに）

＿＿＿＿＿＿＿＿＿＿ borrow your pencil?

★⑥ （焼きそばの作り方を教えてほしいときに）

＿＿＿＿＿＿＿＿＿＿ teach me how to cook fried noodles?

⑦ （宿題がわからないときに）

＿＿＿＿＿＿＿＿＿＿ help me with my homework?

**4** 例にならい，may を使った文を作りなさい。　B

ポイント
**may ~**
「～してもよい，～かもしれない」

（例）　Perhaps she is wrong.

→ She may be wrong.

★① Perhaps she is in the gym.

＿＿＿＿＿＿＿＿＿＿＿＿＿＿＿＿＿＿＿＿＿＿＿＿＿＿

② Perhaps she is not hungry.

＿＿＿＿＿＿＿＿＿＿＿＿＿＿＿＿＿＿＿＿＿＿＿＿＿＿

③ Perhaps Mike is telling lies.

＿＿＿＿＿＿＿＿＿＿＿＿＿＿＿＿＿＿＿＿＿＿＿＿＿＿

④ Perhaps I will not go out tonight.

＿＿＿＿＿＿＿＿＿＿＿＿＿＿＿＿＿＿＿＿＿＿＿＿＿＿

**総合**　日本文を参考に，空所に can か may を補いなさい。

① It (　　　　　　　) snow tomorrow.　（明日は雪かもしれません。）

② (　　　　　　　) you swim across the river?　（その川を泳いで渡れますか。）

③ (　　　　　　　) I smoke here?　（ここでタバコを吸ってもいいですか。）

④ (　　　　　　　) he be an actor?　（彼が俳優なんてことがありうるだろうか。）

⑤ (　　　　　　　) I ask you a question?　（質問をしてもいいですか。）

**21**

# Lesson ⓾ 助動詞（2）

→参考書 p.104-111
→文法書 p.26-27

**1** 例にならい，次の文の後ろに（　　）内の語句を加えて，過去形の文にしなさい。　Ａ

（例）　I must go to meet my uncle at the airport. （yesterday）

　　　→ I had to go to meet my uncle at the airport yesterday.

① I must work part time. （last summer）

- - - - - - - - - - - - - - - - - - - - - - - - - - - - - - - - - - - - - - -

② They must get up at six in the morning. （during the holidays）

- - - - - - - - - - - - - - - - - - - - - - - - - - - - - - - - - - - - - - -

③ Our cousin must wait for us at the station. （then）

- - - - - - - - - - - - - - - - - - - - - - - - - - - - - - - - - - - - - - -

④ People must work so hard to survive. （in those days）

- - - - - - - - - - - - - - - - - - - - - - - - - - - - - - - - - - - - - - -

⑤ Her sister must finish the work by herself. （last week）

- - - - - - - - - - - - - - - - - - - - - - - - - - - - - - - - - - - - - - -

> **ポイント**
> **must ～**
> 「～しなければならない」
> 過去のときはhad to
> ～「～しなければならなかった」を用いる。

**2** 日本文を参考に，[　　]内の語句から適切なものを選んで補いなさい。　Ａ

① You _____ show me your passport here.

（ここでパスポートを見せなくてもいいですよ。）

[must / must not / don't have to]

② Kate _____ help her little brother with his home-work. （ケイトは弟の宿題を手伝わなければならない。）

[must / must not / doesn't have to]

③ Jim looks pale. He _____ be ill.

（ジムは顔色が悪い。気分が悪いにちがいない。）

[must / must not / doesn't have to]

★④ Students _____ use cell phones at school.

（生徒は，学校で携帯電話を使ってはいけません。）

[must / must not / don't have to]

⑤ You _____ tell a lie. （うそをついてはいけません。）

[must / must not / don't have to]

⑥ She'll _____ come back by this time tomorrow.

（彼女は明日のこの時間までに帰って来なければならないでしょう。）

[must / have to / has to]

> **ポイント**
> **must ～**
> 「～しなければならない，～にちがいない」
> **must not ～**
> 「～してはならない」
> **don't have to ～（=**
> **don't need to ～）**
> 「～する必要はない」

**3** 例にならい，「〜すべきでない」の意味の文を２つ作りなさい。　**B**

（例）　eat too much　→ You shouldn't eat too much.
　　　　　　　　　　　→ You ought not to eat too much.

**ポイント**

**should 〜, ought to 〜**
「(当然)〜すべきだ，〜するはずだ」
ought to 〜は否定形に注意 : ought not to 〜(＝shouldn't 〜)

① work too hard

② watch too much TV

③ talk too loudly

④ buy that expensive dress

⑤ study all the time

⑥ drive too fast

**4**　下記の語群から適切なものを選んで，対話文を完成させなさい。　**C**

① *A:* (　　　　) shut the window?　*B:* All right.

② *A:* (　　　　) bring you a chair?　*B:* Yes, please.

③ *A:* (　　　　) have more coffee?
　*B:* No, thanks.  I've had enough.

★④ *A:* (　　　　) go out tonight?　*B:* Yes, let's.
　a. Will you　b. Won't you　c. Shall I　d. Shall we

**ポイント**

**will や shall を使った疑問文**
Will you 〜?「〜してくれませんか」/ Won't you 〜?「〜しませんか」/ Shall I 〜?「〜しましょうか」/ Shall we 〜?「〜しませんか」

**総合**　日本文の意味に合うように，(　　　)内の語句を並べかえて，文を完成させなさい。

① 運転するときは，シートベルトを締めるべきです。
　When you are driving, (a seat belt / you / should / wear).

② 皿洗いをしてくれませんか。　(you / the dishes / will / wash), please?

③ 図書館では大声で話してはいけません。　(not / speak loudly / you / must) in the library.

# Lesson ⑪ 受動態（1）

➡参考書 p.124－126
⟳文法書 p.28－29

**1** 例にならい，次の文を受動態の文にしなさい。 Ａ

（例）　Many young people visit Hiroshima.

→ Hiroshima is visited by many young people.

① Everybody likes Vickie.

--------

② Mary cleans the room every day.

--------

③ Many children enjoy the TV program.

--------

★④ Many people around the world love soccer.

--------

⑤ People in Mexico speak Spanish.

--------

⑥ Mr. Green teaches English.

--------

⑦ Many people eat Japanese food.

--------

> **ポイント**
> **受動態の作り方**
> (1)能動態の目的語
> 　→受動態の主語
> (2)能動態の動詞
> 　→be-動詞＋過去
> 　分詞
> (3)能動態の主語
> 　→by …として後
> ろに置く

**2** 例にならい，次の文を受動態の文にしなさい。 Ａ

（例）　The earthquake destroyed the city.

→ The city was destroyed by the earthquake.

① Shakespeare wrote *Hamlet*.

--------

② My mother took these pictures.

--------

③ My sister made this ring.

--------

④ Picasso painted this picture.

--------

⑤ The sound of rain broke the silence.

--------

⑥ Three boys found the money.

--------

> **ポイント**
> **過去時制の受動態**
> was
> were ｝＋ 過去分詞

**24**

**3** 例にならい，次の文を受動態の文にしなさい。　A

(例)　Do many young people visit Okinawa?

　　　→ Is Okinawa visited by many young people?

① Do cows eat grass?

--------------------------------------------

② Did Vickie wash my car?

--------------------------------------------

③ Mr. Green doesn't teach Spanish.

--------------------------------------------

④ Did your friends help you?

--------------------------------------------

⑤ James didn't use this bike.

--------------------------------------------

**4** 例にならい，下線部を主語とした受動態の文にしなさい。　B

(例)　You find koalas in Australia.

　　　→ Koalas are found in Australia.

① They don't sell stamps in that store.

--------------------------------------------

② Somebody cleans the room every day.

--------------------------------------------

★③ He finished his work before five o'clock.

--------------------------------------------

④ They built the bridge last year.

--------------------------------------------

⑤ We use milk for making butter and cheese.

--------------------------------------------

**総合**　日本文の意味に合うように，(　　)内の語句を並べかえて，文を完成させなさい。

① 多くの事故は不注意な運転によって引き起こされます。

(caused / careless driving / are / many accidents / by).

--------------------------------------------

② ピラミッドは何千年も前に建てられました。

(built / the pyramids / thousands of years ago / were).

--------------------------------------------

③ その車のドアはかぎがかかっていなかった。

The door (locked / not / of / the car / was).

--------------------------------------------

# Lesson ⑫ 受動態(2)

●参考書 p.127-131
●文法書 p.30-31

**1** 例にならい，それぞれの下線部を主語にした2つの受動態の文に書きかえなさい。 A

(例) They gave <u>him</u> <u>a book</u>.

　　　→ He was given a book. / A book was given to him.

① Mr. Long teaches <u>us</u> <u>history</u>.

　We ＿＿＿＿＿＿＿＿＿＿＿＿＿＿＿＿＿ .

　History ＿＿＿＿＿＿＿＿＿＿＿＿＿＿＿ .

② Tom sent <u>Ann</u> <u>a nice present</u>.

　Ann ＿＿＿＿＿＿＿＿＿＿＿＿＿＿＿＿＿ .

　A nice present ＿＿＿＿＿＿＿＿＿＿＿ .

★③ The school lent <u>Jim</u> <u>a new computer</u>.

　Jim ＿＿＿＿＿＿＿＿＿＿＿＿＿＿＿＿＿ .

　A new computer ＿＿＿＿＿＿＿＿＿＿ .

④ James showed <u>me</u> <u>all the pictures</u>.

　I ＿＿＿＿＿＿＿＿＿＿＿＿＿＿＿＿＿＿ .

　All the pictures ＿＿＿＿＿＿＿＿＿＿ .

⑤ Mike sent <u>me</u> <u>the letter</u>.

　I ＿＿＿＿＿＿＿＿＿＿＿＿＿＿＿＿＿＿ .

　The letter ＿＿＿＿＿＿＿＿＿＿＿＿＿ .

> **ポイント**
> 「S＋V＋O₁＋O₂」の文の受動態
> O₁を主語とするもの，O₂を主語とするものの2通りが可能。

**2** 例にならい，下線部を主語にした受動態の文に書きかえなさい。 A

(例) The news made <u>him</u> happy.

　　　→ He was made happy by the news.

① The noise kept <u>me</u> awake all night.

＿＿＿＿＿＿＿＿＿＿＿＿＿＿＿＿＿＿＿＿＿＿＿＿＿＿＿＿

★② My friends call <u>me</u> Dick.

＿＿＿＿＿＿＿＿＿＿＿＿＿＿＿＿＿＿＿＿＿＿＿＿＿＿＿＿

③ They elected <u>Laura</u> class president. （by ...は不要）

＿＿＿＿＿＿＿＿＿＿＿＿＿＿＿＿＿＿＿＿＿＿＿＿＿＿＿＿

④ They named <u>the baby</u> Richard. （by ...は不要）

＿＿＿＿＿＿＿＿＿＿＿＿＿＿＿＿＿＿＿＿＿＿＿＿＿＿＿＿

⑤ The students kept <u>the room</u> clean.

＿＿＿＿＿＿＿＿＿＿＿＿＿＿＿＿＿＿＿＿＿＿＿＿＿＿＿＿

⑥ Somebody left <u>the door</u> open. （by ...は不要）

＿＿＿＿＿＿＿＿＿＿＿＿＿＿＿＿＿＿＿＿＿＿＿＿＿＿＿＿

> **ポイント**
> 「S＋V＋O＋C」の文の受動態
> Oを主語とし，Cは動詞の後にそのまま残す。

**3** 例にならい，次の文を受動態の文にしなさい。　**B**

(例)　We must solve the problem of pollution.

　　→ The problem of pollution must be solved.

ポイント
助動詞を含む文の受動態
助動詞＋動詞の原形
↓
助動詞＋be＋過去分詞

① Somebody will tell you where to go.

② You must take this medicine every day.

③ We shouldn't use this word in formal situations.

★④ They will play many exciting games in the new ballpark.

⑤ You must write the answers on the paper.

⑥ We can see Mt. Fuji clearly from here.

**4** 日本文の意味に合うように，下記の語群から適切なものを選んで記号を記入しなさい。　**C**

ポイント
動作主が by ...以外で表される受動態
1つ1つイディオムとして覚えていこう。

★① だれもがそのニュースに驚いた。

　　Everybody was surprised (　　　　).

② 彼は古い車に興味がある。

　　He is interested (　　　　).

③ 彼女は2等賞に満足していない。

　　She is not satisfied (　　　　).

④ 彼はすぐれた役者としてみんなに知られている。

　　He is known (　　　　) as a good actor.

⑤ この家は木造です。

　　This house is made (　　　　).

　　a. to everyone　　　b. in old cars　　　c. at the news

　　d. of wood　　　　　e. with the second prize

**総合** 日本文の意味に合うように，(　　　　)内の語句を並べかえて，文を完成させなさい。

① そのトロフィーは勝者に与えられました。　(the trophy / to / given / was / the winner).

② その仕事は明日までに終わるだろうか。　(the work / finished / will / be) by tomorrow?

③ 彼の名前は世界中の人々に知られています。

　　(to / known / is / his name / people) all over the world.

# Lesson ⑬ 不定詞（1）

●参考書 p.144-149
●文法書 p.34-35

**1** 下線部が主語・補語・目的語のうちどの働きをしているかを答えなさい。 A

① They decided <u>to go</u> by plane.　（　　　　　　）

② To see is <u>to believe</u>.　（　　　　　　）

③ <u>To obey</u> the laws is everybody's duty.　（　　　　　　）

④ I hope <u>to have</u> a good time at Tom's party.　（　　　　　　）

⑤ My pleasure is <u>to listen</u> to pop music.　（　　　　　　）

⑥ <u>To become</u> a scientist was his dream.　（　　　　　　）

⑦ Don't promise <u>to do</u> it, if you are not sure that you can.

　　　　　　　　　　　　　　　　　　　　　　　（　　　　　　）

> **ポイント**
> to-不定詞(to＋動詞の原形)が名詞としての働きをする場合

**2** 例にならい，斜線の箇所のどちらかに（　　）内の語句を入れて，文を完成させなさい。 A

（例）　It is / important / a promise.　(to keep)

　　　→ It is important to keep a promise.

① He / hoped / a professional soccer player.　(to be)

-------------------------------------------------

② His job / is / students English.　(to teach)

-------------------------------------------------

③ I want / alone / all over Japan someday.　(to travel)

-------------------------------------------------

④ It is fun / a soccer game / at a stadium.　(to watch)

-------------------------------------------------

⑤ Her dream / is / in France.　(to study)

-------------------------------------------------

★⑥ It is dangerous / everything / on the Internet.　(to believe)

-------------------------------------------------

⑦ It is hard / a good library / in this town.　(to find)

-------------------------------------------------

⑧ It was exciting / the famous actor / .　(to meet)

-------------------------------------------------

⑨ It is / very important / English.　(to learn)

-------------------------------------------------

⑩ The plane is / beginning / down the runway.　(to move)

-------------------------------------------------

> **ポイント**
> **名詞の働きをするto-不定詞**
> 主語として，補語として，動詞の目的語としての働きをする。

**3** 例にならい，（　　）内の語句の動詞を不定詞にして前の文につなぎ，文を完成させなさい。　B

（例）　What is the best way?　(learn a foreign language)

→ What is the best way to learn a foreign language?

ポイント
形容詞の働きをする
to-不定詞
名詞の後に続く。

① You should take something.　(read in the train during your trip)

------

② She has a lot of friends.　(support her when she is in trouble)

------

③ He kept his promise.　(help me)

------

④ She has the ability.　(speak three languages)

------

★⑤ Neil Armstrong was the first man.　(walk on the moon)

------

**4** 日本文の意味に合うように，空所に適語を補いなさい。　C

① 100歳まで長生きする人もいます。

Some people live (　　　　　) (　　　　　) one hundred years old.

② 彼は音楽を勉強するためにイタリアに行きました。

He went to Italy in order (　　　　　) (　　　　　) music.

★③ 目が覚めてみると，彼は見知らぬ部屋にいた。

He awoke (　　　　　) (　　　　　) himself in a strange room.

④ 彼は母親に電話をかけるために立ち上がった。

He got up (　　　　　) (　　　　　) his mother.

⑤ その少年は成長して偉大な学者になった。

The boy grew up (　　　　　) (　　　　　) a great scholar.

★⑥ 子どもを起こさないように，彼は静かに入って来た。

He came in quietly so (　　　　　) (　　　　　) (　　　　　) wake the child.

ポイント
副詞の働きをする
to-不定詞
「～するために」(目
的)
「…してその結果
～」(結果)

in order [so as] to
～「～するために」
/ in order [so as]
not to ～「～しない
ように」

**総合** 日本文の意味に合うように，（　　）内の語句を並べかえて，文を完成させなさい。

① 私の父の趣味は庭の花の世話をすることです。

(take / to / is / my father's hobby) care of flowers in our garden.

------

② おなかがすきました。何か食べ物がほしいです。

I'm hungry.　(want / I / to / something / eat).

------

# Lesson ⑭ 不定詞（2）

●参考書 p.149−153
●文法書 p.36−37

**1** 日本文の意味に合うように，空所に適語を補いなさい。 A

① そんなことをするなんて，あなたは不注意でしたね。

You were careless (　　　　　) (　　　　　) that.

② その知らせを聞いてうれしいです。

I am glad (　　　　) (　　　　　) the news.

★③ 家まで車で送ってくださるなんてあなたはとても親切でしたね。

You were very nice (　　　　) (　　　　　) me home.

④ きみはそんな給料のよい仕事を得て運がよかったよ。

You were lucky (　　　　) (　　　　) such a well-paid job.

⑤ あなたのペットの犬が亡くなったと聞いてとても悲しかった。

I was very sad (　　　　) (　　　　　) that your pet dog
had died.

★⑥ このケーキは作るのがとても簡単です。

This cake is very easy (　　　　) (　　　　).

> **ポイント**
> **副詞の働きをする to-不定詞**
> 「〜して」（感情の原因）
> 「〜するとは」（判断の根拠）
> 「〜するのが（…だ）」（形容詞の意味を限定）

**2** 例にならい，（　　）内の語句がto-不定詞の意味上の主語になるように補いなさい。 B

（例） It is dangerous to swim in this river. （children）

　　→ It is dangerous for children to swim in this river.

① It is necessary to learn a foreign language. （us）

-------

② It was kind to come all the way to meet me. （you）

-------

③ It is natural to say so. （him）

-------

④ It was careless to lose your key. （you）

-------

⑤ It is dangerous to run fast. （an old man）

-------

⑥ It was nice to take me to the airport. （you）

-------

⑦ It was impossible to find the cap. （the boy）

-------

⑧ It is not easy to write good English. （me）

-------

> **ポイント**
> for / of を使ってto-不定詞の意味上の主語を表す。
> **It is ... for A to 〜**
> 「Aが〜することは…だ」
> **It is ... of A to 〜**
> 「〜するとは A は…だ」

**3** 例にならい，文を完成させなさい。 C

（例）　Don't go.　(I told him …)
　　→ I told him not to go.

① Do your best.　(I want you …)

-----

② Stay home.　(She asked me …)

-----

③ Don't use too much sugar.　(She advised him …)

-----

④ He will win the race.　(I expect him …)

-----

⑤ She is a genius.　(I think her …)

-----

> **ポイント**
> **tell＋O＋to-不定詞**
> 「Oに～しなさいと言う」
> **want＋O＋to-不定詞**
> 「Oに～してもらいたい」
> **ask＋O＋to-不定詞**
> 「Oに～してほしいと頼む」
> to ～の動作をするのはOである。

**4** 日本文の意味に合うように，(　　　)内の語句を並べかえて，文を完成させなさい。 C

① 医者は彼に働きすぎないようにと忠告した。
　The doctor (him / work / advised / not to) so hard.

> **ポイント**
> 「S＋V＋O＋to-不定詞」の語順に注意する。

② 母は私に買い物に行くように頼んだ。
　Mother (me / go / asked / to) shopping.

-----

③ 私たちがここにいることをだれにも知られたくない。
　We (anybody / don't want / know / to) that we're here.

-----

④ あなたが手伝ってくれたらもっと早く仕事が終わるでしょう。
　Your help will (me / finish / to / enable) my job sooner.

-----

⑤ 彼は自分の家の中ではだれにもタバコを吸わせない。
　He doesn't (anyone / allow / smoke / to) in his house.

-----

**総合** 日本文の意味に合うように，空所に適語を補いなさい。

① この質問は答えるにはとても難しい。
　This question is very difficult (　　　　　) (　　　　　).

② 私はあなたに数日間私の赤ん坊の世話をしてもらいたい。
　I (　　　　　) you (　　　　　) look after my baby for a few days.

③ そんな簡単な間違いをするなんてあなたは不注意でしたね。
　It was careless (　　　　　) (　　　　　) to make such a simple mistake.

# Lesson ⑮ : 不定詞（3）

●参考書 p.154-158
●文法書 p.38-39

**1** 例にならい，（　）内の語句を並べかえて，文を完成させなさい。　A

（例）　I (cross / saw / the man) the road.

→ I saw the man cross the road.

① Mr. Green (his son / made / wash) the car.

② My father (go / let / me) camping with Jim.

③ Mary (carry / had / Tom) her heavy baggage upstairs.

④ I didn't (come / hear / you) in.

⑤ I (felt / shake / the house).

⑥ She (get off / the passengers / watched) the bus.

★⑦ They (saw / get / Tom) into his car.

> **ポイント**
> 使役動詞＋O＋動詞の原形
> 「Oに〜させる，させてやる」
> 知覚動詞＋O＋動詞の原形
> 「Oが〜するのを知覚する」

**2** 例にならい，文を作りなさい。　A

（例）　Bob entered his room. → I saw Bob enter his room.

★① We ran every day.

The coach made _____ .

② The students went home.

The teacher let _____ .

③ He came here at five.

I had _____ .

④ Something touched his cheek.

He felt _____ .

⑤ He came into our room.

We heard _____ .

⑥ The sun came up.

I watched _____ .

⑦ Children talked.

She liked to listen to _____ .

> **ポイント**
> Oの次にくる動詞は原形であることに注意。

**3** 例にならい，次の文を〈too ... to 〜〉か〈... enough to 〜〉を用いて書きかえなさい。　**B**

> ポイント
>
> too ... to 〜 は否定の意味を含む。
> 「〜するには…すぎる，…すぎて〜できない」
> ... enough to 〜 は肯定の意味を含む。
> 「〜できるほど…だ，…なので〜できる」

(例)　My grandmother is so old that she cannot drive a car.

　　→ My grandmother is too old to drive a car.

　　Are you so hungry that you can eat two hamburgers?

　　→ Are you hungry enough to eat two hamburgers?

① I was so tired that I could not get up this morning.

　I was ................................................................ .

② The boy was so tall that he could touch the ceiling.

　The boy was ................................................................ .

★③ My grandmother is so old that she cannot travel alone.

　My grandmother is ................................................................ .

④ She is not so old that she can get married.

　She is not ................................................................ .

⑤ She is so old that she can travel by herself.

　She is ................................................................ .

⑥ He is so fat that he cannot dance.

　He is ................................................................ .

**4**　各文の(　　)内に，[　　]内から適語を選んで補いなさい。　**C**

> ポイント
>
> 疑問詞＋to-不定詞
> 「何を[いつ，どこで，など]〜すべきか」
> what to 〜 / who to 〜 / which to 〜 / when to 〜 / where to 〜 / how to 〜 / whether to 〜 (or not)

① I don't know (　　　　　) to do next.　[why / what / who]

② Will you tell me (　　　　　) way to go?

　[which / where / how]

③ Could you advise me (　　　　　) to go or not?

　[where / whether / why]

④ Have you decided (　　　　　) to leave here?

　[when / where / why]

⑤ I'll ask (　　　　　) to get there.　[where / how / which]

⑥ I found out (　　　　　) to buy fruit cheaply.

　[where / what / which]

**総合**　日本文の意味に合うように，空所に適語を補いなさい。

① 彼女はまだ外出できるほど元気ではありません。

　She isn't well (　　　　　) (　　　　　) go out yet.

② 夕食に何を作るか決めましたか。

　Have you decided (　　　　　) (　　　　　) (　　　　　) for dinner?

③ 何があなたの心を変えたのですか。

　What (　　　　　) you (　　　　　) your mind?

# Lesson ⓰ 動名詞

文法書 p.40-41

**1** 下線部が主語・補語・目的語のうちどの働きをしているかを答えなさい。 **A**

① Traveling abroad is a lot of fun. （　　　　　）

★② Her share is cleaning the living room. （　　　　　）

③ My uncle has given up smoking. （　　　　　）

④ Did you finish painting your house? （　　　　　）

⑤ Eating too much makes me sleepy. （　　　　　）

⑥ I don't mind waiting a few minutes. （　　　　　）

> **ポイント**
> **動名詞**
> 名詞の働きをする〜
> ing 形
> 文中で主語・補語・
> 目的語として働く。

**2** 例にならい，日本文の意味に合うように，（　　　）内の前置詞の後に動詞の形を変えて続け，文を完成させなさい。 **A**

（例） ジムはだれにもさよならを言わずに部屋から出て行った。

Jim left the room. （without / say goodbye to anyone）

　→ Jim left the room without saying goodbye to anyone.

> **ポイント**
> 前置詞の後に「〜す
> ること」を続けると
> きは必ず動名詞にな
> る。to-不定詞にこ
> の用法はない。

① 私はいつも出勤前に朝食をとる。

I always have breakfast. （before / go to work）

- - - - - - - - - - - - - - - - - - - - - - - - - - - - - - - - - -

② パーティーにお招きいただき，ありがとうございます。

Thank you. （for / invite me to the party）

- - - - - - - - - - - - - - - - - - - - - - - - - - - - - - - - - -

③ 間違いをすることを心配してはいけません。

Don't worry. （about / make a mistake）

- - - - - - - - - - - - - - - - - - - - - - - - - - - - - - - - - -

★④ 私は英語を話すときに間違うのが怖い。

I'm afraid. （of / make mistakes when I speak English）

- - - - - - - - - - - - - - - - - - - - - - - - - - - - - - - - - -

⑤ 彼女は自分でお金を払うと主張した。

She insisted. （on / pay for herself）

- - - - - - - - - - - - - - - - - - - - - - - - - - - - - - - - - -

⑥ 彼は外国語を学ぶことに興味があります。

He is interested. （in / learn foreign languages）

- - - - - - - - - - - - - - - - - - - - - - - - - - - - - - - - - -

⑦ 私は仕事に行かず一日中寝ていた。

I stayed in bed all day. （instead of / go to work）

- - - - - - - - - - - - - - - - - - - - - - - - - - - - - - - - - -

**3** ( )内の動詞を動名詞かto-不定詞にしなさい。 A

① She enjoys (play) tennis. _____

② We've decided (leave) here. _____

③ The boys refused (listen) to me. _____

④ He wants (become) an artist. _____

⑤ He promised (help) me. _____

⑥ Would you mind (help) me carry this box? _____

⑦ Where have you decided (go)? _____

⑧ Have you finished (clean) the kitchen? _____

⑨ You should stop (work) so hard. _____

⑩ She was only pretending (be) asleep. _____

**4** 日本文の意味に合うように，( )内から動名詞かto-不定詞のいずれかを選びなさい。 B

① 私はあなたの手紙を忘れずに投函するつもりです。

I'll remember (to post / posting) your letter.

② 私は以前どこかで彼女に会った覚えがある。

I remember (to see / seeing) her somewhere before.

③ 宿題をするのを忘れるな。

Don't forget (to do / doing) your homework!

④ 私は富士山を初めて見たことをけっして忘れないでしょう。

I'll never forget (to see / seeing) Mt. Fuji for the first time.

⑤ 私は逆立ちをしようとしたが，できなかった。

I tried (to stand / standing) on my head, but I couldn't.

⑥ 私は逆立ちをしてみたが，頭が痛くなった。

I tried (to stand / standing) on my head, but it gave me a headache.

⑦ 残念ながら私はあなたを助けることはできません。

I regret (to say / saying) that I cannot help you.

⑧ 14歳で学校をやめたことを私は後悔しています。

I regret (to leave / leaving) school at fourteen.

**総合** 日本文の意味に合うように，空所に適語を補いなさい。

① 彼はうまく入学試験に合格することができた。

He succeeded ( ) ( ) the entrance exam.

② 私はついにその申し出を受け入れることに決めました。

I finally ( ) ( ) ( ) the offer.

③ きみは外出するときに明かりを消し忘れましたね。

You ( ) ( ) ( ) off the lights when you went out.

# Lesson ⑰ 分詞(1)

➡参考書 p.186-190
➡文法書 p.42-43

**1** 日本文の意味に合うように，（　）内の動詞を現在分詞か過去分詞に直しなさい。　A B

① そのシャンプーの容器は再生されたプラスチックでできている。

　The shampoo bottle is made of (recycle) plastic.　＿＿＿＿＿＿

② レストランで食事をしていた人たちはみんな観光客でした。

　All the people (eat) in the restaurant were tourists.

　＿＿＿＿＿＿

③ あなたは今までにその笑っている女の子に会ったことがありますか。

　Have you ever met that (smile) girl?　＿＿＿＿＿＿

④ 床に壊れたおもちゃの車がありました。

　There was a (break) toy car on the floor.　＿＿＿＿＿＿

⑤ これらは私の母が焼いたクッキーです。

　These are the cookies (bake) by my mother.　＿＿＿＿＿＿

★⑥ 戦っている男の人たちはとても大きい。

　The (fight) men are very big.　＿＿＿＿＿＿

> **ポイント**
> **名詞を修飾する分詞**
> 現在分詞「〜している…」
> 過去分詞「〜された…」

**2** 例にならい，次の2つの文を分詞を使って1つの文にしなさい。　A B

（例）Do you know the boys?  They are playing in the park.
　→ Do you know the boys playing in the park?

① I discovered a book.  The book was written by my father.

＿＿＿＿＿＿＿＿＿＿＿＿＿＿＿＿＿＿＿＿＿＿＿＿

② The woman is my teacher.  She is walking across the street.

＿＿＿＿＿＿＿＿＿＿＿＿＿＿＿＿＿＿＿＿＿＿＿＿

③ I talked to the man.  He was selling food.

＿＿＿＿＿＿＿＿＿＿＿＿＿＿＿＿＿＿＿＿＿＿＿＿

④ I spoke to the woman.  She was standing on the corner.

＿＿＿＿＿＿＿＿＿＿＿＿＿＿＿＿＿＿＿＿＿＿＿＿

⑤ The tests were very difficult.  They were given to the students.

＿＿＿＿＿＿＿＿＿＿＿＿＿＿＿＿＿＿＿＿＿＿＿＿

★⑥ The girl is my sister.  She is practicing kendo over there.

＿＿＿＿＿＿＿＿＿＿＿＿＿＿＿＿＿＿＿＿＿＿＿＿

⑦ There are a lot of food.  They are imported from USA.

＿＿＿＿＿＿＿＿＿＿＿＿＿＿＿＿＿＿＿＿＿＿＿＿

> **ポイント**
> 分詞が名詞を修飾するとき，分詞のみ単独でなければ，後ろから修飾する。

**3** 例にならい，（　）内の語を用いて文を作りなさい。　C

（例）　She was reading a book.　(sat)

　　　　→ She sat reading a book.

① He was surprised at the news.　(seemed)

--------------------------------------------------

② The people were looking at the beautiful picture.　(stood)

--------------------------------------------------

③ The treasure was hidden in the castle.　(lay)

--------------------------------------------------

④ She was encouraged by her parents' kind words.　(felt)

--------------------------------------------------

⑤ She was tired from working so hard all day.　(felt)

--------------------------------------------------

> ポイント
> **S＋V＋分詞**
> S＝Cの関係に注意。

**4** 例にならい，文を作りなさい。　C

（例）　He was lying in front of the sofa.

　　　　→ She found him lying in front of the sofa.

① He was working very hard.

　　I found _____.

★② His car was unlocked.

　　He left _____.

③ The garden gate is closed.

　　Please keep _____.

④ The water was running in the bathtub.

　　Someone left _____.

⑤ He was waiting for a while in the classroom.

　　Mr. Green kept _____.

> ポイント
> **S＋V＋O＋分詞**
> O＝Cの関係に注意。

**総合** 日本文の意味に合うように，（　）内の語句を並べかえて，文を完成させなさい。

① バイオリンを弾いている少年はジムです。

　(the boy / the violin / playing / Jim / is).

--------------------------------------------------

② 人々は，試合の間ずっと興奮したままだった。

　(people / excited / remained / during the game).

--------------------------------------------------

③ そのドアにかぎをかけないままにしておいてはいけない。

　(you / leave / mustn't / unlocked / the door).

--------------------------------------------------

# Lesson ⑱ 分詞(2)

➲参考書 p.194-197
➲文法書 p.44-45

**1** 例にならい，第1文を分詞構文に変えて，第2文と結んで1文にしなさい。 **A**

(例) She heard the doorbell. She ran to open the door.

→ Hearing the doorbell, she ran to open the door.

① She entered the room. She found them reading comic books.

- - - - - - - - - - - - - - - - - - - - - - - - - - - - - - - - - - - - - -

② She was satisfied with the result. She praised the student.

- - - - - - - - - - - - - - - - - - - - - - - - - - - - - - - - - - - - - -

③ He was shocked by the news. He couldn't speak a word.

- - - - - - - - - - - - - - - - - - - - - - - - - - - - - - - - - - - - - -

④ She looked backward. She saw a man following her.

- - - - - - - - - - - - - - - - - - - - - - - - - - - - - - - - - - - - - -

★⑤ This book is written in easy English. This book is suitable for beginners.

- - - - - - - - - - - - - - - - - - - - - - - - - - - - - - - - - - - - - -

⑥ He was poor. He could not afford to buy books.

- - - - - - - - - - - - - - - - - - - - - - - - - - - - - - - - - - - - - -

> **ポイント**
> **分詞構文**
> 同じ主語・同じ時制で表される2つの文の一方を，分詞で始まる句で表現する。

**2** 下線部に注意して，次の各文を日本語に直しなさい。 **B**

★① The boy rowed the boat, <u>singing a song</u>.

- - - - - - - - - - - - - - - - - - - - - - - - - - - - - - - - - - - - - -

② <u>Having a map</u>, we didn't lose our way.

- - - - - - - - - - - - - - - - - - - - - - - - - - - - - - - - - - - - - -

③ <u>Seeing his master</u>, the dog began to bark happily.

- - - - - - - - - - - - - - - - - - - - - - - - - - - - - - - - - - - - - -

④ <u>Having a lot of things to do</u>, he stayed home.

- - - - - - - - - - - - - - - - - - - - - - - - - - - - - - - - - - - - - -

⑤ The old man lived alone, <u>forgotten by everybody</u>.

- - - - - - - - - - - - - - - - - - - - - - - - - - - - - - - - - - - - - -

⑥ <u>Raising her hand</u>, she asked a question.

- - - - - - - - - - - - - - - - - - - - - - - - - - - - - - - - - - - - - -

⑦ <u>Walking along the street</u>, I found a nice restaurant.

- - - - - - - - - - - - - - - - - - - - - - - - - - - - - - - - - - - - - -

> **ポイント**
> **分詞構文と主たる文の意味のつながり**
> 同時に起こることがら「～しながら」/時「～していたときに」/連続して起こることがら「～して」/理由「～なので」

**3** 例にならい，下線部を分詞構文に直して，全文を書きなさい。　**A** **B**

（例）　Because he felt very hungry, Mike ordered a double hamburger.

→ Feeling very hungry, Mike ordered a double hamburger.

**ポイント**

**分詞構文の作り方**
(1)接続詞をとる。
(2)主語をとる。
(3)動詞を分詞にする。
能動態の文は現在分詞で，受動態の文は過去分詞で始める。

① When she found her lost ring, she jumped for joy.

② Because I knew that he was poor, I offered to pay his fare.

③ When she looked out of the window, she saw a rainbow.

④ As we live in the country, we have very few visitors.

⑤ Because he was tired from work, he went to bed early.

⑥ When the earth is seen from the moon, it must look like a ball.

⑦ We stood chatting for one hour and we forgot to go shopping.

★⑧ Because I had nothing to do, I watched TV.

⑨ As he heard a noise, he looked toward the door.


**総合**　日本文の意味に合うように，（　　）内の語句を並べかえて，文を完成させなさい。

① 私たちは彼の到着を待ちながら，夜遅くまで起きていた。

We stayed awake until late, (for / his arrival / waiting).

② 大統領は，みんなの支持を受け，将来に自信を持っていた。

The President, (all the people / by / supported), felt confident about the future.

③ 彼女は，母親に付き添われて入って来た。

She came in, (her mother / accompanied / by).

④ その町で道に迷ったので，私は交番を探しました。

(lost / in / getting / the town), I looked for a police box.

# Lesson ⑲ 比較（1）

参考書 p.210-215
文法書 p.46-47

**1** 次の比較変化表を完成させなさい。　A

| | 原級 | 比較級 | 最上級 |
|---|---|---|---|
| ① | | larger | |
| ② | | | longest |
| ③ | great | | |
| ④ | big | | |
| ⑤ | | | easiest |
| ⑥ | difficult | | |
| ⑦ | early | | |
| ⑧ | | | least |
| ⑨ | | prettier | |
| ⑩ | much | | |

> **ポイント**
> 不規則な変化をする語に注意。

**2** 日本文の意味に合うように，空所に適語を補いなさい。　B

★① 私はあなたと同じくらいうれしいです。

I'm (　　　　　　) (　　　　　　) (　　　　　　) you.

② この馬はあの馬と同じくらい速く走ります。

This horse runs (　　　　) (　　　　) (　　　　)
that horse.

③ 昨日ほど寒くありません。

It isn't (　　　　) (　　　　) (　　　　) yesterday.

④ 私の兄はジョンほどテニスが上手ではありません。

My brother doesn't play tennis (　　　　) (　　　　)
(　　　　) John.

⑤ はちみつは，砂糖とほぼ同じくらい甘い。

Honey is just about (　　　　) (　　　　) (　　　　)
sugar.

⑥ この時計はあの時計と同じくらい高価です。

This watch is (　　　　) (　　　　) (　　　　) that
one.

⑦ 彼女は見かけほど年をとっていない。

She is (　　　　) (　　　　) old (　　　　) she looks.

⑧ 彼は私と同じくらい本を持っています。

He has (　　　　) (　　　　) books (　　　　) I
have.

> **ポイント**
> **A ... as＋原級＋as B**
> 「AはBと同じぐらい〜である」
> **A ... not as [so]＋原級＋as B**
> 「AはBほど〜でない」

**40**

**3** 日本文の意味に合うように，（　）内の語を並べかえて，文を完成させなさい。　C

① あなたのアパートは私のアパートよりずっと大きい。

Your apartment is (than / larger / much) mine.

ポイント
比較級を強める語句
much, far, a lot,
even, still

② 私はマイクよりずっとゆっくり歩いた。

I walked (more / than / slowly / much) Mike.

③ 馬は犬よりもずっと速く走ることができる。

Horses can run (than / much / faster) dogs.

④ 私には，英語のほうが科学よりずっとおもしろい。

To me, English is (more / much / interesting / than) science.

**4** 例にならい，（　）内の語句を適切な位置に補って，文を完成させなさい。　C

（例）　He is younger than I.　(two years)

　　→ He is two years younger than I.

① Tom is older than Jim.　(one year)

ポイント
数量を表す語句を比
較級の前に置いて，
程度の差を具体的に
表す。
three years older
than A「Aより3歳年
上」

★② My father is older than my mother.　(three years)

③ Bill is heavier than his brother.　(five pounds)

④ That cord is longer than this one.　(eighty centimeters)

⑤ This train leaves earlier than that one.　(ten minutes)

⑥ John is taller than his father.　(two inches)

**総合** 各組の文がほぼ同じ内容を表すように，空所に適語を補いなさい。

①
{ Basketball is not as popular as tennis.
{ Tennis is (　　　　　) (　　　　　) (　　　　　) basketball.

②
{ Money is not as important as health and happiness.
{ Health and happiness are (　　　　　) (　　　　　) (　　　　　) money.

③
{ John is fifteen years old.　His brother is ten years old.
{ John is five years (　　　　　) (　　　　　) his brother.

# Lesson ⑳ 比較(2)

➡参考書 p.216-219
➡文法書 p.48-49

**1** 日本文の意味に合うように，(　　)内の語句を並べかえて，文を完成させなさい。 **A**

> **ポイント**
> the＋最上級＋in [of]
> …
> 「…の中で一番～」

① キリマンジャロはアフリカで一番高い山です。

Kilimanjaro is (highest / the / in Africa / mountain).

------

② このホテルが町で一番安いです。

This hotel is (town / cheapest / in / the).

------

③ フィレンツェが私の国では最も美しい都市です。

Florence is (in my country / the / city / most beautiful).

------

★④ メアリーは私たちのクラスの中で一番背が高い女の子です。

Mary is (in our class / tallest / the / girl).

------

⑤ 大阪は日本で2番目に大きな都市だ。

Osaka is (second largest / the / city / in Japan).

------

⑥ 東京スカイツリーは日本で一番高いタワーです。

Tokyo Skytree is (in Japan / tallest / the / tower).

------

**2** 日本文の意味に合うように，空所に適語を補いなさい。 **A**

> **ポイント**
> { in＋場所・集団
> { of＋複数のもの
> much や by far をつけて最上級を強調することができる。

★① ボブはすべての科目の中で歴史が一番好きだ。

Bob likes history (　　　　　) (　　　　　) (　　　　　) all
subjects.

② バーミンガムはイギリスで2番目に大きい都市です。

Birmingham is the (　　　　　) (　　　　　) city (　　　　　)
Britain.

③ この曲はそのアルバムの中でとび抜けて人気があります。

This song is (　　　　　) (　　　　　) the most popular on
the album.

④ 私の兄はクラスで一番速く走ります。

My brother runs (　　　　　) (　　　　　) (　　　　　) his
class.

**3** 例にならい，次の各文がほぼ同じ内容を表すように，空所に適語を補いなさい。 **B**

(例) Mt. Everest is the highest mountain.

　a. No other mountain is (as) high (as) Mt. Everest.
　b. No other mountain is (higher) than Mt. Everest.
　c. Mt. Everest is (higher) than (any) (other) mountain.

**ポイント**
最上級の意味合いは，原級，比較級を用いて表せる。

★① Alaska is the largest state in the USA.

　a. No other state in the USA is (　　　　　) large (　　　　　) Alaska.
　b. No other state in the USA is (　　　　　) than Alaska.
　c. Alaska is (　　　　　) than (　　　　　) (　　　　　) state in the USA.

② Mary is the tallest girl in the class.

　a. No other girl in the class is (　　　　　) tall (　　　　　) Mary.
　b. No other girl in the class is (　　　　　) than Mary.
　c. Mary is (　　　　　) than (　　　　　) (　　　　　) girl in the class.

③ This is the funniest story that I have ever heard.

　a. I have never heard (　　　　　) a funny story (　　　　　) this.
　b. I have never heard a (　　　　　) story than this.

④ Mary is the prettiest girl that I have ever seen.

　a. I have never seen (　　　　　) a pretty girl (　　　　　) Mary.
　b. I have never seen a (　　　　　) girl than Mary.

**総合** 日本文の意味に合うように，(　　　　)内の語句を並べかえて，文を完成させなさい。

① あなたの国で一番人気のあるスポーツは何ですか。

What (is / popular sport / the / most) in your country?

- - - - - - - - - - - - - - - - - - - - - - - - - - - - - - - - - - - - - - - - - - - - - - - - - - -

② 富士山は日本のほかのどの山よりも高い。

Mt. Fuji (than / is / higher / other / any / mountain) in Japan.

- - - - - - - - - - - - - - - - - - - - - - - - - - - - - - - - - - - - - - - - - - - - - - - - - - -

③ それは私が今までに食べた中でずば抜けて一番ひどい料理だった。

That was (the / by far / worst / dish) I'd ever had.

- - - - - - - - - - - - - - - - - - - - - - - - - - - - - - - - - - - - - - - - - - - - - - - - - - -

**1** 例にならい，次の2つの文を関係代名詞を使って1つの文にしなさい。 A

(例) This is the man. He wanted to see you.

　　 → This is the man who wanted to see you.

★① I have a friend. He / She lives in Spain.

-------

② Do you know anybody? He / She wants to buy a car.

-------

③ Correct the sentences. They are wrong.

-------

④ He always wears clothes. They are too small for him.

-------

⑤ The man was a friend of yours. He telephoned.

-------

> **ポイント**
> 第2文の代名詞を関係代名詞にして第1文につなぐ。
> 先行詞が「人」：who
> 先行詞が「物」：which

**2** 例にならい，次の2つの文を1つの文にしなさい。 B

(例) The dress is very pretty. You are wearing it.

　　 → The dress you are wearing is very pretty.

① The books are my brother's. I lent them to you.

-------

② Did you get the pictures? I sent them to you.

-------

③ This is the story. He wrote it.

-------

④ The man is my father. You met him yesterday.

-------

⑤ Fall is the season. I like it best of all.

-------

⑥ The flowers are still fresh. I cut them this morning.

-------

⑦ This is the book. You wanted it.

-------

⑧ The teacher gave me some advice. I visited her yesterday.

-------

> **ポイント**
> 目的格の関係代名詞は省略されることが多い。

**3** 例にならい，次の２つの文を関係代名詞を使って１つの文にしなさい。 **C**

(例) I met a girl. Her parents worked in a hospital.

→ I met a girl whose parents worked in a hospital.

ポイント
関係代名詞who,
whichの所有格：
whose

★① Do you know anyone? His / Her dream is like mine.

-------------------------------------------------

② That dictionary is Bob's. Its cover is red.

-------------------------------------------------

③ That's the man. His house has burned down.

-------------------------------------------------

④ We met the man. His son won the race.

-------------------------------------------------

⑤ That book is for people. Their first languages are not English.

-------------------------------------------------

**4** 例にならい，次の２つの文を関係代名詞 that を使って１つの文にしなさい。 **D**

(例) Don't believe anything. He says it.

→ Don't believe anything that he says.

ポイント
関係代名詞thatが好
んで用いられる場合
先行詞が「唯一」
　the only ...,　the
　same ...,　　the
　very　 ...,　　the
　first ...,　　the＋
　最上級
先行詞が「全・無」
　all ...,　every ...,
　any ...,　no ...

① These are all things. We know them.

-------------------------------------------------

② The captain was the last person. He left the sinking ship.

-------------------------------------------------

③ This is the same watch. I bought it in Tokyo.

-------------------------------------------------

④ We must do everything. We can do it.

-------------------------------------------------

⑤ This is the most famous book. I know it.

-------------------------------------------------

⑥ I will give you everything. You want it.

-------------------------------------------------

**総合** 次の文の( )内から適切な関係代名詞を選びなさい。

① This is the longest novel (whom / that) I have ever read.

② What's the name of the man (whose / who) car you borrowed?

③ The number of tourists (whom / who) visit Bali is increasing.

④ The bird (which / whom) was injured by a cat will get well soon.

⑤ Did you get the things (which / whom) you wanted?

⑥ This is a word (which / whose) meaning I don't know.

# Lesson ㉒ 関係詞（2）

文法書 p.54-55

**1** 例にならい，日本語の部分にwhatを用いて英語に直し，文を完成させなさい。　**A**

（例）　（あなたがしたこと）is the right thing.

　　→ What you've done is the right thing.

> **ポイント**
> what「…すること[もの]」
> それ自体に先行詞を含んでいる。

① He got （彼のほしいもの）.

--------

② Is this （あなたが探しているもの）?

--------

③ Were you surprised at （彼が言ったこと）?

--------

④ I cannot do （彼が私にしてほしいこと）.

--------

⑤ （彼の言うこと） is not important.

--------

⑥ （彼が一番好きなこと） is just sitting in the sun.

--------

⑦ Please show me （あなたが買ったもの）.

--------

**2** 日本文の意味に合うように，空所に適切な関係副詞を補いなさい。　**B**

① 月曜日が私のひまな日です。

　　Monday is the day （　　　　　　　） I am free.

② 私が働いているビルの中に託児所があります。

　　There is a day-care center in the building （　　　　　　　） I work.

> **ポイント**
> 関係副詞
> 「場所」を表す語句
> ＋where …
> 「時」を表す語句＋
> when …

③ あそこが交通事故のあった場所ですか。

　　Is that the place （　　　　　　　） the traffic accident happened?

*④ 私たちが昼食を食べたレストランは地図には載っていません。

　　The restaurant （　　　　　　　） we ate lunch is not on the map.

⑤ 彼女は，その地震があった年に生まれた。

　　She was born in the year （　　　　　　　） the earthquake occurred.

⑥ 冗談を言ってはいけないときがある。

　　There are times （　　　　　　　） you must not tell a joke.

⑦ いつの日か，私は子ども時代を過ごした町へ行きます。

　　One day I'm going to the town （　　　　　　　） I spent my childhood.

**3** 日本文を参考に，次の文の（　　）内から適切なほうを選びなさい。　**B**

① Paris is the city (where / which) I want to live.

（パリは，私が住んでみたい街です。）

② She lives in a house (where / which) is 100 years old.

（彼女は築100年の家に住んでいる。）

③ This is the room (where / which) I work.

（ここが，私が仕事をする部屋です。）

④ Sunday is the day (when / which) I get up late.

（日曜日は私が寝坊する日です。）

⑤ The office (where / which) is on the second floor is small.

（２階にある事務所は狭い。）

⑥ The city (where / which) we spent our vacation was beautiful.

（私たちが休暇を過ごした町は美しかった。）

★⑦ I'll never forget the summer (when / which) I traveled to France.

（私は，フランスへ旅をした夏をけっして忘れないでしょう。）

ポイント
先行詞が「場所」「時」を表す語句であっても，関係詞が導く節の中で代名詞の働きをしていれば関係代名詞を用いる。

**4** 例にならい，文を作りなさい。　**C**

（例）　He didn't come for this reason.

→ This is why he didn't come.

① The war broke out for that reason.

--------------------------------------------------

② He was late for this reason.

--------------------------------------------------

③ She said nothing about the matter for this reason.

--------------------------------------------------

④ He made a mistake for this reason.

--------------------------------------------------

ポイント
関係副詞why ...は先行詞なしで用いられることがある。
**This is why ...**「こういうわけで…」
**That is why ...**「そういうわけで…」

**総合** 日本文の意味に合うように，（　　）内の語句を並べかえて，文を完成させなさい。

① ものごとは，見かけとは違う。　Things are (what / look / they / not).

--------------------------------------------------

② 彼はいつも学生時代のことばかり話している。

He is always talking about (the days / was / when / he) a student.

--------------------------------------------------

③ ここが，私が２年前から働いている会社です。

This is (I / the office / have been working / where) for two years.

--------------------------------------------------

# Lesson ㉓ 仮定法

➡参考書 p.282-285
➡文法書 p.56-57

**1** 例にならい，[ ]内の語を適切な形に直して，仮定法の文を作りなさい。 A

(例) I am sick. If I (were) not sick, I (could) go with you.
　　[be / can]

① I don't have enough time. If I (　　　　　) enough time, I
　(　　　　　) see you off at the airport. [have / can]

② That book is expensive. If that book (　　　　　) not
　expensive, I (　　　　　) buy it. [be / will]

③ He speaks too fast. If he (　　　　　) more slowly, people
　(　　　　　) understand him. [speak / can]

④ I am not a good cook. If I (　　　　　) a good cook, I
　(　　　　　) make all of my own meals. [be / will]

⑤ There is no telephone here. If there (　　　　　) one, we
　(　　　　　) call them up. [be / can]

★⑥ Tom isn't here. If Tom (　　　　　) here, I (　　　　　)
　explain it to him myself. [be / can]

⑦ I don't speak French. If I (　　　　　) French, my job
　(　　　　　) be much easier. [speak / will]

> **ポイント**
> **仮定法過去**
> 現在の事実の反対の仮定
> If+S+過去形 ..., S +助動詞の過去形＋動詞の原形 ...

**2** 例にならい，[ ]内の語を適切な形に直して，仮定法の文を作りなさい。 B

(例) I was tired. If I (had) not (been) so tired, I would (have)
　　(gone) out. [be / go]

① I didn't have a camera. If I (　　　　　) (　　　　　) a
　camera, I would (　　　　　) (　　　　　) some pictures.
　[have / take]

② She had a headache. If she (　　　　　) not (　　　　　) a
　headache, she would (　　　　　) (　　　　　) with us.
　[have / come]

③ You didn't ask me for tickets. If you (　　　　　) (　　　　　)
　me for tickets, I could (　　　　　) (　　　　　) some.
　[ask / get]

④ I didn't know you were in the hospital. If I (　　　　　)
　(　　　　　) you were in the hospital, I would (　　　　　)
　(　　　　　) you there. [know / visit]

> **ポイント**
> **仮定法過去完了**
> 過去の事実の反対の仮定
> If+S+had＋過去分詞 ..., S＋助動詞の過去形＋have＋過去分詞 ...

**3** 例にならい，次の各文を〈I wish＋仮定法〉の文に書きかえなさい。 C

> **ポイント**
> **I wish＋仮定法の文**
> 「…であればなあ」
> 「願望」を表す。

（例） I can't speak Spanish.

→ I wish I could speak Spanish.

① I don't like dancing.

--------

② You were not here yesterday.

--------

③ I don't know his address.

--------

④ I didn't study hard.

--------

⑤ I'm not rich.

--------

⑥ They didn't work hard.

--------

**4** 日本文の意味に合うように，（　　）内の語句を並べかえて，文を完成させなさい。 D

> **ポイント**
> **If＋S＋should ～**
> 「もしも万が一Sが
> ～すれば」
> ありそうもないこと
> の仮定

① 万が一また失敗したら，あなたはどうしますか。

(if / again / fail / should / you), what will you do?

--------

② 万が一明日雨が降れば，私たちは出発を延ばします。

(if / tomorrow / rain / should / it), we'll put off our departure.

--------

③ 万が一彼が電話をしてきたら，私は家にいないと言ってください。

(if / call / he / should), tell him I am not at home.

--------

④ 万が一その仕事につくように言われたら，私はその仕事につくと思います。

(if / the job / I / be offered / should), I think I would take it.

--------

**総合** 日本文の意味に合うように，空所に適語を補いなさい。

① もし私があなただったら，そんなことはしないだろう。

If I (　　　　　　　) you, I (　　　　　　　) not (　　　　　　　) such a thing.

② 万が一彼が遅れるようなことがあれば，私たちは彼を残して出発しなければならなくなります。

If he (　　　　　　　) be late, we'll have to start without him.

③ あんなにお金を使わなかったらなあ。

I wish I (　　　　　　　) (　　　　　　　) so much money.

# Optional Lesson 1　接続詞

➡参考書 p.234–247
⤵文法書 p.58–59

**1** 日本文の意味に合うように，（　　）内から適切なものを選びなさい。　A C

① 彼女はあまり背は高くありませんが，バスケットボールが上手です。

　She is not very tall, (and / but / for) she is a good basketball player.

② こちらに来てみてください。そうすれば花火がもっとよく見えますよ。

　Come here, (and / but / or) you can see the fireworks better.

③ よく勉強しなさい。そうしないと数学の試験に落ちますよ。

　Work hard, (and / or / but) you will fail your test in math.

④ 彼は起きるのが遅い。だからいつも学校に遅れる。

　He is a late riser, (but / for / so) he is always late for school.

⑤ 彼女は早く寝ました。というのも疲れていたからです。

　She went to bed early, (and / for / but) she was tired.

⑥ 私たちはちょうど今はそんなに忙しくないのだから，休憩したらいいよ。

　(Since / Until) we're not very busy just now, you can take a rest.

⑦ もしあまり疲れていなければ，あなたと魚釣りに行きます。

　(When / Unless) I am too tired, I'll go fishing with you.

⑧ ロンドンにいるときは，ふつう私は演劇を見に行きます。

　(Because / When) I'm in London, I usually go to the theater.

⑨ あなたが行かせてくれるまで私は叫ぶのをやめませんよ。

　I won't stop shouting (until / when) you let me go.

⑩ おじいさんは80歳を超えているのに，まだとても元気にしている。

　(Although / Because) Grandpa is over eighty, he is still very active.

> **ポイント**
>
> **接続詞**：文と文を結びつける。
> A and B
> 「AそしてB」
> A but B
> 「AしかしB」
> A or B「AまたはB」
> A, so B
> 「A，だからB」
> A, for B「A，というのはBだから」

**2** Aの文と意味がつながるように，Bから適切なものを選んで結びなさい。　B C

| A | B |
|---|---|
| ① I'll go there | ア．since I came here. |
| ② His story is true | イ．though it may appear strange. |
| ③ I'll help you | ウ．that we could walk on it. |
| ★④ It is nice | エ．unless it rains. |
| ⑤ I'll wash this dress | オ．that tomorrow is a holiday. |
| ⑥ The ice was so thick | カ．so that you can wear it. |
| ⑦ I cannot understand him | キ．because he speaks too fast. |
| ⑧ It is ten years | ク．if I can. |

> **ポイント**
>
> 主節と従属節の意味のつながりに注目。

# Optional Lesson 2 : 話法

→参考書 p.299-301
→文法書 p.60-61

**1** 例にならい，直接話法を間接話法に書きかえなさい。 **A**

（例） He said, "I can't swim." → He said that he couldn't swim.

★① Tom said, "I have a stomachache."

--------------------------------

② She said, "I like my new hairstyle."

--------------------------------

③ She said, "I did it."

--------------------------------

④ He said to me, "I'll drive you home."

--------------------------------

⑤ She said, "I have given up my job."

--------------------------------

⑥ She said, "My parents are very well."

--------------------------------

⑦ The teacher said to me, "You did well on the test."

--------------------------------

> **ポイント**
> 平叙文の話法転換
> said, "...."
> ↓
> said (that) ....
>
> said to 人, "...."
> ↓
> told 人 (that) ....

**2** 例にならい，直接話法を間接話法に書きかえなさい。 **B**

（例） She said to me, "Will you marry me?"
  → She asked me if I would marry her.

① They said to me, "Can you help us?"

--------------------------------

② She said to me, "How do you know my name?"

--------------------------------

③ I said, "When does the last train leave?"

--------------------------------

④ She said to me, "Is there any food in your house?"

--------------------------------

⑤ She said to me, "Does my hair look funny?"

--------------------------------

⑥ She said to me, "Am I doing the right thing?"

--------------------------------

⑦ She said to me, "How many books do you want?"

--------------------------------

> **ポイント**
> 疑問文の話法転換
> Yes / No-疑問文
> ↓
> asked（人）if [whether]
> ＋S＋V
>
> 疑問詞疑問文
> ↓
> asked（人）疑問詞＋
> S＋V

**1** 例にならい，数えられる名詞にa / anを，数えられない名詞に×をつけなさい。 A

(例) ① a teacher  ② × milk  ③ an eye

① ____ bread     ② ____ orange     ③ ____ student
④ ____ umbrella  ⑤ ____ sugar      ⑥ ____ dog
⑦ ____ water     ⑧ ____ child      ⑨ ____ hour
⑩ ____ artist    ⑪ ____ dictionary ⑫ ____ money

> **ポイント**
> a [an] は数えられる名詞の前につく。
> a＋子音で始まる語
> an＋母音で始まる語

**2** 例にならい，空所に適切な代名詞を補いなさい。 B

(例) Is this your coat?
　　 —— Yes, it is (my) coat. It belongs to (me). It is (mine).

① Is this my money? —— Yes, it is (　　　　　　) money. It belongs
　 to (　　　　). It is (　　　　　　).

② Is this her book? —— Yes, it is (　　　　　　) book. It belongs to
　 (　　　　). It is (　　　　　　).

③ Is this your house? —— Yes, it is our house. It belongs to
　 (　　　　). It is (　　　　　　).

④ Is this their dog? —— Yes, it is (　　　　　　) dog. It belongs to
　 (　　　　). It is (　　　　　　).

> **ポイント**
> 「人」を表す代名詞は人称の変化に注意。

**3** 例にならい，(　　)内に-self [-selves] を補って対話文を完成させなさい。 B

(例) Did you have a nice time at the party?
　　 —— Yes, I enjoyed (myself) at the party.

① Did you and your wife have a nice time during the vacation?
　 —— Yes, we enjoyed (　　　　　　) during the vacation.

② Did Dick have a good time yesterday?
　 —— Yes, he enjoyed (　　　　　　) yesterday.

③ Did the children have a nice time on the beach?
　 —— Yes, they enjoyed (　　　　　　) on the beach.

> **ポイント**
> oneselfの形の変化に注意。
> myself / yourself /
> himself / herself /
> itself / ourselves /
> yourselves / them-
> selves

**4** 例にならい，質問に肯定または否定で答えなさい。 C

(例) Do you have a pen?
　　 —— Yes, I have one. / No, I don't have one.

① Do you have a dictionary? —— No, _____.

② Do you have a bicycle? —— Yes, _____.

> **ポイント**
> 名詞のくり返しを避けるためのone
> 「a [an] ＋既出名詞」
> の代わりをする。

**1** （　　）内の語を適切な場所に入れて，文を完成させなさい。また，日本語に訳しなさい。　**A**

★① Sally has eyes.　(green)

訳：

② You must keep your hands.　(clean)

訳：

③ There isn't milk in the fridge.　(much)

訳：

④ I have money with me.　(little)

訳：

> **ポイント**
> **形容詞の用法**
> 名詞を修飾したり，補語となる。

**2** 意味が通るように，（　　）内の語句を並べかえて，文を完成させなさい。　**A**

① We arrived (early / at / the party).

② I opened (quietly / the door / very).

③ They (at 7 o'clock / have dinner / usually).

④ Tom (read / slowly / the letter).

> **ポイント**
> **副詞の位置**
> 「頻度」・「否定」を表すもの：否定文を作るときのnotと同じ位置
> その他のもの：自動詞の後，「他動詞＋目的語」の後

**3** 日本文の意味に合うように，空所に適切な前置詞を補いなさい。　**B**

① バス停にはだれもいません。

There is nobody (　　　　　　　) the bus stop.

② 彼は私たちの家に来ました。　He came (　　　　　　　) our house.

③ アレックスは1977年から1985年までカナダに住んでいました。

Alex lived in Canada (　　　　　　) 1977 (　　　　　　) 1985.

④ 彼らは結婚して10年になる。

They've been married (　　　　　) ten years.

⑤ 電車は数分後に出発します。

The train will leave (　　　　　) a few minutes.

> **ポイント**
> **前置詞**
> それぞれの基本的な意味を覚えておこう。

→参考書 p.386-401
↪文法書

**1** 下線部に注意して，日本語に訳しなさい。　A B

① Not all children like apples.

--------

② I am not always free on Sundays.

--------

③ *A:* I hope we'll meet again.

　*B:* So do I.

　*A:* _____

　*B:* _____

④ If she doesn't go, neither will I.

--------

> **ポイント**
> **部分否定**
> 「すべてが…である わけではない(なか には…でないものも ある)」の意味合いを 表す。
> **倒置構文**
> So＋V＋S「…もそ うだ」
> Neither [Nor]＋V＋ S「…もそうでない」

**2** 例にならい，下線部を強調した構文を作りなさい。　B

(例)　Tom met Mary at the bookstore.

　→ It was Mary that Tom met at the bookstore.

① Tom met Mary at the bookstore.

--------

② Tom met Mary at the bookstore.

--------

③ Tina teaches mathematics to young children.

--------

④ Tina teaches mathematics to young children.

--------

⑤ Tina teaches mathematics to young children.

--------

> **ポイント**
> **強調構文**
> It is ... that ～.
> 強調したい部分を It isとthatの間に置 き，残りをthatの後 ろに続ける。

**3** 空所に，下の[　]内から適切なものを選んで補いなさい。　C

① Do you want to have a (　　　　　) at my photos?

② Let's take a (　　　　) and have some coffee.

③ Can I have a (　　　　) on your bike?

④ The baby gave a (　　　　) as her mother walked away.

⑤ *A:* I can't open the plastic bottle.

　*B:* Here, let me have a (　　　　).

　[break / cry / look / ride / try]

> **ポイント**
> have [take, make, give, get]＋a＋動作 を表す名詞

**4** 例にならい，（　　）内の動詞を用いて文を完成させなさい。　**D**

ポイント

無生物主語構文
「…が人を〜する」→
「…のために人は〜
する」

（例）　If you drink this tea, you will sleep well.　(help)
　　　→ This tea will help you sleep well.

① We all laughed at his jokes.　(make)

　　His jokes _____ .

② A rabbit's ears are so large that it can hear the slightest sound.
　　　　　　　　　　　　　　　　　　　　　　　　(enable)

　　A rabbit's ears _____ .

③ Why are you so angry with her?　(make)

　　What _____ ?

④ Because of a broken leg, he couldn't play in the game.　(keep)

　　A broken leg _____ .

★⑤ If you have a good sleep, you will feel better.　(make)

　　A good sleep _____ .

⑥ He couldn't sleep well because of the noise of the traffic.　(keep)

　　The noise of the traffic _____ .

⑦ Many people like him because of his honesty.　(make)

　　His honesty _____ .

⑧ The plants grow thanks to solar energy.　(make)

　　Solar energy _____ .


**5** 日本文の意味に合うように，空所に適語を補いなさい。　**D**

ポイント

無生物主語構文によ
く用いられる動詞を
覚えておこう。

★① 天気が悪かったので，私たちは外出できなかった。

　　The bad weather (　　　　　　) us (　　　　　　) going out.

② この道を行けば湖に着くでしょう。

　　This road will (　　　　　　) you to the lake.

③ 彼女が手伝ってくれれば，もっと早く仕事を済ませられるでしょう。

　　Her help will (　　　　　　) me to do the job sooner.

④ コーヒーを飲んだために私はほとんど一晩中眠れなかった。

　　The coffee (　　　　　　) (　　　　　　) awake almost all night.

⑤ コーチの助言に助けられてチームは勝利をおさめた。

　　The coach's advice (　　　　　　) the team to win.

⑥ 食べ物のにおいをかいで，私はおなかがすいてきた。

　　The smell of food (　　　　　) (　　　　　　) hungry.

⑦ 私はこれらの写真を見ると学生時代を思い出す。

　　These pictures (　　　　) me (　　　　　　) my school days.

# 品詞と文法用語のまとめ

## ▶▶ 品詞

英文を構成する単語は，それぞれの働きによって主に次の7つの品詞に分類されます。

| 名 | 名　詞 | 人や事物の名前を表す。<br>**Naoko** comes to **school** by **bike**.　（ナオコは自転車で通学します。） |
|---|---|---|
| 代 | 代名詞 | 名詞の代わりに用いられる。I, we, you, he, she, it, theyなど。<br>**She** knows **him**.　（彼女は彼を知っています。） |
| 動 | 動　詞 | 主語の後に続いて，「～します」や「～です」を表す。<br>I **play** tennis every day.　（私は毎日テニスをします。） |
| 形 | 形容詞 | 名詞を修飾したり，主語を説明したりする。<br>She is **happy**.　（彼女は幸せです。） |
| 副 | 副　詞 | 主として動詞を修飾する。<br>Listen to me **carefully**.　（注意して聞きなさい。） |
| 前 | 前置詞 | 名詞や代名詞の前に置かれて，ひとまとまりの意味を表す。<br>at, by, for, in, from, of, on, to, withなど。 |
| 接 | 接続詞 | 語と語，句と句，文と文を結びつける。<br>and, but, or, that, because, when, while, ifなど。 |

## ▶▶ 文法用語

| be-動詞 | 「…です」にあたるam, are, is, was, were。 |
|---|---|
| 一般動詞 | be-動詞以外のすべての動詞。 |
| 自動詞 | 動作の対象(目的語)を必要としない動詞。 |
| 他動詞 | 動作の対象(目的語)を必要とする動詞。 |
| 現在分詞 | 動詞の～ing形。進行形を作ったり，名詞を修飾したりする。 |
| 過去分詞 | 動詞の-ed形(不規則変化あり)。受動態や完了形を作ったり，名詞を修飾したりする。 |
| 知覚動詞 | 「見る」「聞く」など感覚を表す動詞。see, watch, hear, listen to, feel, noticeなど。 |
| 使役動詞 | 「～させる」という意味の動詞。make, let, have, getなど。 |
| 形式主語 | to-不定詞やthat-節などの代わりに，本来の主語の位置に置かれるitのこと。<br>**It** is dangerous to believe everything on the Internet.<br>（インターネット上のすべてのことを信じるのは危険です。） |
| 形式目的語 | to-不定詞やthat-節などの代わりに，本来の目的語の位置に置かれるitのこと。<br>I found **it** easy to ride a horse.　（私は馬に乗るのは簡単だとわかった。） |

**訂正情報配信サイト** 17143-01

❶利用については，先生の指示にしたがってください。

❷利用に際しては，一般に，通信料が発生します。

https://dg-w.jp/f/d4814

# Zoom English Grammar 23 Lessons

## WORKBOOK THIRD EDITION

| | |
|---|---|
| 2004年1月10日　初版　　第1刷発行 | 編　者　第一学習社編集部 |
| 2022年1月10日　改訂3版　第1刷発行 | 発行者　松本洋介 |
| | 発行所　株式会社　第一学習社 |

東京：〒102-0084　東京都千代田区二番町5番5号　☎03-5276-2700

大阪：〒564-0052　吹田市広芝町8番24号　☎06-6380-1391

広島：〒733-8521　広島市西区横川新町7番14号　☎082-234-6800

札　幌☎011-811-1848　　仙　台☎022-271-5313　　新　潟☎025-290-6077

つくば☎029-853-1080　　東　京☎03-5803-2131　　横　浜☎045-953-6191

名古屋☎052-769-1339　　神　戸☎078-937-0255　　広　島☎082-222-8565

福　岡☎092-771-1651

**書籍コード**　17143-01　　＊落丁・乱丁本はおとりかえいたします。

　　　　　　　　　　　　　　　　解答は個人のお求めには応じられません。

ISBN978-4-8040-3003-6　　　ホームページ　　http://www.daiichi-g.co.jp/